Building Your Own PC

Buying and Assembling with Confidence

Arnie Lee

Abacus

Credits	
Managing Editor	Scott Slaughter
Technical Editor	Jim Oldfield, Jr.,
Illustrations	Melinda Thede
Photography	Arnie Lee & Melinda Thede
Cover Art & Design	Melinda Thede

Acknowledgments

Thanks to Scott who turned plain text into a very readable book.

Thanks to Melinda who drew some top notch illustrations for this book on such short notice.

Thanks to Jim who added a lot of "usability" suggestions to the text.

Thanks to Rachel and Michael and Jennifer and Karla who helped at many of the computer shows where we "researched" this project.

And thanks to the rest of the family who made it without us for so many weekends.

Dedication

This book is dedicated to our son Scott.

As I see it, he probably wouldn't need this book.
Instead, he'd figure out how to build one himself.

Contents

Contents

Introduction

This book is for you if -

❖ You'd like to build a screaming fast Pentium computer

❖ You'd like to have advice on selecting and buying the best components

❖ You'd like to have step-by-step instructions on assembling your new PC

❖ You'd like to save money

❖ You'd like to be able to later upgrade your computer to keep it up to date

Since you're already reading this book, we know that you're very interested in building your own PC. This book isn't your typical computer book. This is a "roll up your sleeves and get your hands dirty" kind of book. You'll find it to be short and to the point.

This book's step-by-step instructions make it possible for you to put together your own personal computer. And you don't have to be an electronics whiz to build your own. We'll show you how to select components, connect them together and install the software that you'll need to get your PC up and running so that you can put it into action.

Figure I-1 The Pentium 166 system in this minitower case has a CD-ROM and sound card. It was assembled in about an hour and is now ready for action

Introduction

The information we've presented here is based on many years of experience with PCs. We've seen several generations of personal computers come and go. And we've seen many different features, peripherals and devices come and go. As they've come and gone, we've spent a lot of time and money investing in technology that turned out to be short-lived. We want to help you avoid this mistake yourself.

Just like the classic Archie Bunker Show, this book is loaded with opinions. However, we'd like to think that these opinions are educated ones. We'll show you how to build your own PC at a rock bottom price. You'll have the satisfaction of saving money and knowing how to repair and upgrade your computer when the time comes.

There are an infinite number of ways to combine different components to make a personal computer. But we're going to show you how to build a PC based on one of the Intel Pentium processors. If you've been keeping up with the latest technology, you'll know that Cyrix makes a Pentium-clone known as the 6x86 CPU. For our discussion, the Cyrix 6x86 CPU is equivalent and interchangeable with a Pentium processors.

Of course there are other choices. For example, you can find good buys on Intel 486 CPUs, or one of the AMD or Cyrix 586 processors. But we believe that in today's fast changing marketplace, the smartest choice is a Pentium PC. And with all the power sitting in your new system, you'll be able to run any of today's power-hungry Windows and Windows 95 applications with ease.

How much can you save? Unfortunately, we can't give you an exact answer. The amount of money that you save depends on many factors: the features that you want in your custom built computer, the quality of the components that you select, the amount of time you spend shopping for these components, the competitiveness of the personal computer marketplace and how well you're able to bargain with salespeople.

For the computer that we're putting together in this book, we saved about $600 to $800 compared to one with similar features that you can buy from a discount computer store. We bought components from several local computer stores, computer superstores and from vendors at several of the many weekend computer shows. You can save even more if you are a better shopper than us.

We hesitate to put prices in this book because they have changed so quickly in recent months. Luckily for us, they have always moved towards **lower** prices.

Because there are so many features and add-ons that you can build into a PC, it isn't possible to talk about every different combination.

Therefore, we have to draw some boundaries. We won't be able to show you how to build every kind of Pentium computer system, but we will show you how to build a PC with these characteristics:

❖ Pentium CPU

❖ 3.5" floppy drive

❖ IDE hard drive

❖ Plug 'n' Play sound card

❖ IDE CD-ROM drive

❖ PCI video display card

❖ Monitor

❖ Windows 95

After putting this computer together, we know that you'll have both the skills and the confidence to "upgrade" this new computer with virtually any other add-ons that you may want. Since we have to limit the scope of this book, we won't be able to cover all of these peripherals here. So if you're planning to add a modem or a tape backup, you'll be able to do so on your own.

How long does it take to build a PC? Not long at all. The computer pictured in Figure I-1 was assembled in about an hour. If you already have all of the components, you can assemble your first computer in less than three hours and install the operating system in another hour. However, you will spend a lot more time than two hours evaluating, selecting and buying the components. The Shopping Check List in Chapter 6 will help you cut your non-assembly time to a minimum.

It's a good idea to read through this book entirely before you start building your computer. By doing this, you'll become very familiar with the way in which you'll be putting your computer together. If you have questions after reading a section of the book, you can ask one of the sales people or vendors to clarify the area which isn't crystal clear.

Well enough introductions. Let's get going.

1

The Components
Of A Computer

1 The Components Of A Computer

A personal computer is a lot like an automobile. We all know that there are many different makes and models of automobiles. Some have small, economy engines and others have large, very powerful engines; some have AM/FM radios, others tape cassette decks and still others CD players; some have standard suspensions and others have heavy duty towing packages. But regardless of the options which you buy, automobiles are basically used for transportation.

Figure 1.1 Some autos are built for speed . . . . . And so are some computers

Similarly, there are many different makes and models of personal computers. Some have economy priced CPUs and others more expensive superfast CPUs; some have a minimal 4MB of memory and others are loaded with a hefty 32MB; some have low-cost 2X speed CD-ROM drives and others 8X; some have 8-bit sound cards and others 32-bit wave table sound cards. Regardless of the features, PCs are basically used to run applications.

The components which you choose to put into your PC are similar to the options which you choose for your automobile. Choosing from among different components determines how your PC performs just as choosing from among the various options determines how your automobile performs.

Selecting the right component is important for two reasons:

1. The choice of components ultimately determines how your PC performs.

2. The choice of components also determines how much your PC costs.

We're big advocates of helping you to save money. But don't try to save money at the expense of inferior quality. We'll show you how to build a quality system. Examine your budget, use a prepared shopping list and accept only straight answers to the questions that you ask a sales person. If you follow these guidelines, you'll save money and build the PC that meets your needs. Buy what you need, not what the store or vendor has to sell.

A Bare Bones Computer

Before we go any farther, let's look at the components in a "stripped down" computer. These are the minimal components that all personal computers are made from:

Case

The box or shell in which all of the other components are assembled. The case is typically made of metal, plastic or a combination of the two.

Power supply

provides the electrical power for the other components. Most often, the power supply is included when you buy the case.

CPU

The "Central Processing Unit" is the brain of the PC. Choosing a CPU is the single most important factor in how powerful your PC will be. As we stated in the Introduction, we'll be looking only at Pentium CPUs in this book.

CPU cooling fan

A small unit with a fan that sits on top of the CPU to remove the heat.

Motherboard

A large circuit board which "holds" most of the other components. The CPU, memory, video cards, hard, floppy and CD-ROM drives and other input/output cards fit into the motherboard.

Main memory

Small plug-in cards containing RAM (Random Access Memory) used by programs as working storage. Memory is often called SIMMs. This stands for Single Inline Memory Module which is a fancy name for the way in which the memory is packaged on small circuit boards.

Video display card

A small plug-in card containing specialized chips which generate the signals for displaying text and graphics on the video monitor.

Monitor

The video display device that looks like a television on which the text and graphics appear.

I/O card

Another small plug-in card containing the electronics for controlling the hard drives, floppy drives, communication ports, printer port and game port. There are two major types of I/O cards: IDE and SCSI. In this book, we'll refer only to IDE controllers and not the higher performance (and more expensive) SCSI controllers.

Floppy drive

The device that reads and writes from/to floppy disks.

Keyboard

The device that lets you to type information into the computer.

Many readers have the notion that assembling a computer is very complex. In fact, it's not at all complex. To show you that it's actually quite simple, we assembled the computer system in Figure 1.2 on the top of a table so you can see that there are very few "connections" involved. We used all of the components listed above (except for the case) to make this "bare bones" computer system.

Figure 1.2 We "built" this computer on the top of a table. It runs as well as a computer that you'd build inside a case

This is a real working computer system and runs just like one enclosed in a case. We don't however, recommend that you build your computer on a tabletop. One of the hazards of doing this is that it's very easy to short circuit the motherboard or one of the add-on cards when you don't have a computer case to protect the other components. Short circuiting a delicate component will probably ruin it.

Figure 1.3 (below) shows the connections between the components.

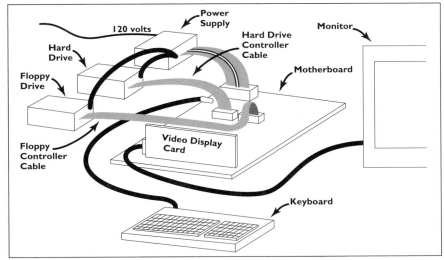

Figure 1.3 This simplified diagram shows how the components in Figure 1.2 are connected

A State Of The Art "Screamer"

Of course none of you will be very satisfied with a bare bones PC. To turn this basic machine into a "state of the art" computer, you can add various features such as the ones we've listed below. These components will turn a basic PC to turn it into a real Pentium screamer:

Cache memory

This is either a small card or several small chips that act as an ultrafast path for moving data between the CPU and main memory.

Hard drive

A device for holding megabytes (millions of bytes) or gigabytes (billions of bytes) of information. A hard drive not only has more capacity than a floppy drive, but reads and writes data dozens of times faster.

CD-ROM drive

A device which reads CD-ROMs, circular plastic discs, that are used to hold programs and information. CD-ROMs provide an economical and convenient way to distribute large programs and huge amounts of data.

Sound card

A plug-in card which can capture, digitize and playback sound. The sound may be music, voices or effects in either monaural or stereo.

Speakers

Similar or identical to audio stereo speakers for amplifying and/or playing the digitized sound generated by a sound card.

Modem

A plug-in card (or in the case of an external modem, a small box) which converts digital information into a form that can be sent back and forth over ordinary telephone lines. A modem is used to connect one computer to another computer in different locations.

Tape backup

A device that uses a small plastic tape cartridges. The cartridges are used to store data that is originally written to the hard drive. By copying or backing up the data from the hard drive to the tape cartridge, the data is saved in case the original data on the hard drive is destroyed.

Mouse

A small hand device used to interact with the graphical user interfaces such as Windows 3.x and Windows 95.

Other peripherals

There are many other peripherals or devices that you can attach to your PC. These includes printers, scanners, zip drives, bar code readers and the list goes on. Installing most of these other peripherals are straightforward and have little to do with building your PC, we'll leave it to others to explain.

2

Selecting The Right Components

2

Selecting The Right Components

Selecting components is probably the single most confusing and time consuming part of building your own PC. There are so many different factors to consider when buying components. When you start shopping for components, you may be bewildered by the myriad of different choices available in every category. Try not to feel overwhelmed. We're going to point you in the right direction.

Here some of the factors that you'll want to consider when you buy the components to build your computer:

The CPU

Earlier we said that the single most important factor in the determining the performance of your PC is which CPU you choose. Basically there are two categories of CPUs: those made by Intel and those by other manufacturers. Since we've decided to build a Intel Pentium PC, we'll simply ignore the non-Intel category.

We've already advised you to invest in an Intel Pentium CPU. However, wherever you shop for components, you'll be able to find bargain priced 486 CPUs. Why not buy a 486? The answer is simple. Why should you invest in technology that's yesterday's? Forget the 486s. Go for a Pentium.

Having made this decision, selecting a CPU is merely a tradeoff between price and performance.

The power rating of a CPU is based on its "clock speed". This is because the work that a CPU can perform is paced by the speed of its internal clock. The faster the clock runs, the more work that the CPU can get done; therefore a more powerful computer.

The clock speed of a CPU is measured in "megahertz" or MHz which stands for millions of cycles per second - pretty darn fast. A Pentium CPU with a higher clock speed is more powerful than a CPU with a lower clock speed. As you would expect, the more powerful CPUs cost more than the less powerful ones.

Figure 2.1 The bottom and top sides of a new Pentium MMX chip, the "engine" of your computer. The CPU on the right is a Pentium "clone" made by Cyrix. For all intents and purposes it runs just like a Pentium

As we go to press again (April, 1997), the typical "starter system" is powered by a 120MHz Pentium CPU. You can of course find systems that use a 100MHz system, but the 120MHz is now the most common CPU in starter systems. Table 2.2 lists the street prices of Pentium CPUs as of April 1997. These prices will most certainly change downward as time goes on, but the table shows you that for a few additional dollars, you get an incremental increase in performance.

Table 2.2			
Street prices of Pentium CPUs (as of April, 1997)			
Intel CPU	Street Price		Street Price
Pentium 75MHz	$100	Pentium MMX 166MHz	$450
Pentium 100MHz	$125	Pentium MMX 200MHz	$675
Pentium 120MHz	$135		
Pentium 133MHz	$160		
Pentium 150MHz	$200		
Pentium 166MHz	$300		
Pentium 200MHz	$550		

Intel recently introduced the Intel MMX CPUs. These new processors are designed to speed performance of multimedia and graphics applications. Currently, most applications are not yet able to take advantage of the speed enhancements, but this should change in the next six months as new versions of popular applications and games are rewritten for the MMX processors.

Cyrix's C6x86 CPUs are targeted at users who want better performance at a better price. Cyrix has cleverly named their processors to complete with Intel's Pentiums. As Table 2.3 shows, Cyrix's C6x86 P120+ runs at an internal clock speed of only 100MHz. However, benchmark tests show that the performance of this CPU exceeds that of a Pentium 120 CPU. Similarly, the C6x86 P200+ runs at a clock speed of only 150MHz yet performs better than a Pentium 200. While there may be some disagreement over which CPU is better, Cyrix does offer an alternative to Intel's Pentiums. The C6x86 CPUs are plug compatible with the Pentium CPU, meaning that the ZIF socket on the motherboard will accommodate either manufacturer's processor.

Table 2.3		
Street prices of Cyrix C6x86 CPUs (as of April 1997)		
Cyrix CPU	Clock Speed	Street Price
C6x86 P120+	100MHz	$120
C6x86 P133+	110MHz	$140
C6x86 P150+	120MHz	$150
C6x86 P166+	133MHz	$190
C6x86 P200+	150MHz	$275

We've found that many Pentium motherboards will accept the C6x86 processors. These motherboards require special jumper settings to handle the different clock speeds and voltage requirements of the Cyrix CPUs. The Cyrix CPUs also include their own CPU cooling fans since they tend to run "hotter" than the Intel processors.

For a better performing PC, buy a faster CPU. But don't spend the kids' lunch money for that increased performance. If you can't afford one of the faster Pentiums today, you can always upgrade to a faster CPU tomorrow. When your checkbook is feeling healthier, you can replace yesterday's 100MHz Pentium CPU with tomorrow's newer and faster 166MHz by simply removing the slower one from the motherboard and inserting the faster CPU.

The prices of CPUs have been falling quite rapidly and most industry watchers predict that they'll continue to drop in price. But waiting for the prices to fall means that you won't be able to use the computer today. Our advice - don't put off that purchase. Sure it may be cheaper tomorrow, but you'll also be delaying the fun, pleasure and utility of using that new computer today. So don't wait too long!!!

Motherboards

The motherboard is a large circuit board that accepts the CPU, memory, plug-in peripheral cards, various connectors and the supporting circuitry for the system.

Selecting a motherboard is the most crucial component that you'll have to buy. Based on our experience advising other computer builders, you'll have more questions about selecting a motherboard that any other component. There are many different makes and models of motherboards. In a computer store or at a computer show, you'll likely find dozens of different motherboards for sale. Most of them are made in Taiwan, Korea or China where the manufacturing costs are among the lowest in the world. And since so many companies make motherboards, there's a lot of competition which means high quality and low prices. That's good for us as consumers.

Figure 2.4 A typical Pentium motherboard like this one has four ISA slots, four PCI slots, four 72-pin SIMM sockets and a cache socket

How do you decide which motherboard to buy?

Note On Motherboards

For the most part, the specific features provided by any motherboard are determined by which *chipset* is used on that motherboard. A chipset provides the supporting circuitry to control most of the other components on the motherboard. In earlier computers such as the "ancient" 386, the functions of the chipset were performed by many separate integrated circuits or chips. Each chip controlled a very specific function such as refreshing the dynamic RAM memory or regulating the high speed DMA transfer to and from a hard drive. But in today's computers, a chipset (usually a set of two to four highly integrated chips) replaces the numerous separate chips.

The two main benefits of chipsets are:
1. The motherboards are less prone to problems
2. The motherboards are less expensive

We've listed criteria on the following pages that you'll want to consider in selecting a motherboard. But as you'll see, your selection will be in part predetermined by which chipset is used on any particular motherboard.

Select a motherboard that will accommodate the type and speed of your CPU

We've already decided to build a Pentium, so we'll choose a motherboard that supports the Pentium CPU. Some Pentium motherboards are built to handle CPU speeds up to 133MHz. The latest motherboards can handle clock speeds of up to 200MHz. If you're looking to use an Intel MMX CPU, make sure that the motherboard can handle its 2.8 voltage requirement.

Since you're a wise shopper, buy a motherboard that will be able to work with these faster CPUs.

If you're looking to install a Cyrix 6x686 200MHz CPU, make sure that its capable of operating at a bus speed of 75MHz.

Select a motherboard that has the type of system bus that you prefer

There are two choices: the PCI bus and the VL-Bus, but only one of them is the right one. Your choice determines which type of add-in cards (such as the video display card) you'll use in your computer. The VL-Bus (VESA Local bus) was originally designed to be used with the 486 processors. Plug-in cards for the VL-Bus are capable of transferring data to and from the CPU at much higher speeds than the original AT bus, a performance limitation left over from the 286 computers.

However, almost all of the new motherboards use the PCI bus. It is the most popular bus today because Intel has put a lot of effort into making this a "standard". The PCI bus is capable of transferring data 64-bit at a time at rates up to 66MHz. Some motherboards, called combos, can simultaneously accommodate add-on cards for both the PCI bus and VL-Bus, so if you need to use both types of cards in your PC, choose one of these combo motherboards. In addition to PCI bus slots and VL-bus slots, all motherboards also have slots for older ISA or EISA plug-in cards as well. This lets you use the "legacy" 8-bit and 16-bit ISA cards and 32-bit EISA cards in your new PC.

A typical Pentium motherboard has three or four slots for PCI or VL-bus cards and three of four slots for ISA/EISA cards. The PCI bus is now a defacto standard for Pentium systems, so we recommend a PCI bus motherboard for simplicity, wide availability of other peripheral cards and future expansion capabilities.

Select a motherboard based on whether you want onboard I/O

A motherboard with onboard I/O, has the built-in electronics for controlling fixed drives, floppy drives, communication ports, a parallel port and usually a game port. Buying a motherboard with onboard I/O, means that you won't have to buy a separate add-on board for handling the I/O. Onboard I/O also frees up one of the slots on the motherboard, a factor worth considering if your case is small or you are planning to add a lot of peripheral cards. Make sure that the onboard I/O has these characteristics: EIDE (Enhanced IDE) interface capable of handling 4 fixed drives and 2 floppy drives, one parallel and two high speed serial communications ports using 16550 UARTs for faster, more reliable data transfer.

Select a motherboard which supports *pipeline burst cache*

Caching is a way to speed up access to main memory. Using standard cache, four bytes of data can be transferred from cache to the CPU in eight clock cycles. A special feature of the Pentiums is its ability to access memory in *burst* mode where the same four bytes of data can be transferred in only five clock cycles. On some motherboards, the cache is already built-in. On other motherboards, the cache is added separately. The more recent motherboards accept a type of cache called COAST memory. COAST is an acronym for <u>C</u>ache <u>O</u>n <u>A</u> <u>ST</u>ick - a clever name for the small circuit boards which accommodate the pipeline burst cache memory.

Select a motherboard which supports the type and amount of memory that you're likely to use

Most Pentium motherboards have four sockets which accept 72-pin SIMMs. Since a single 72-pin SIMMs vary in capacity of from 4MB to 32MB, a motherboard with four sockets can have anywhere from 8MB (using two 4MB SIMMS) to 128MB (using four 32MB SIMMs). If you need more memory, look for a motherboard that has six or more 72-pin SIMM sockets.

Some motherboards also have sockets to accept the older 30-pin SIMMs. If you're on a tight budget and have a considerable amount of money invested in 30-pin SIMMS, then you can extend your investment in this older memory by selecting a motherboard that has sockets for both 30-pin memory <u>and</u> 72-pin memory. Otherwise, we recommend buying a motherboard that accommodates only 72-pin SIMMs.

Most of the Pentium motherboards are able to take advantage of the faster EDO memory. You should select one of these motherboards even if you aren't initially planning to use EDO memory. Many users prefer to buy non-parity memory. If you are one of those who like the security which parity memory offers, make sure that the motherboard supports parity checking.

Following are the major chipsets used on Pentium motherboards. When you're selecting a motherboard, you can easily know which features the motherboard supports based on which chipset is used on that motherboard.

Acer Labs Aladdin chipset

- ❖ PCI bus only with ISA support
- ❖ I/O onboard
- ❖ Keyboard controller
- ❖ Up to 1MB of write-back pipeline burst cache
- ❖ Parity and non-parity memory up to 768MB; supports EDO memory

Figure 2.5

Intel Triton FX chipset

- ❖ PCI bus with ISA support
- ❖ I/O onboard for up to 4 IDE devices
- ❖ Pipeline burst cache
- ❖ Non-parity only memory up to 128MB; supports EDO memory
- ❖ Power management

Figure 2.6

Intel Triton II HX chipset

- ❖ PCI bus with ISA support
- ❖ I/O onboard for up to 4 IDE drives
- ❖ Pipeline burst cache
- ❖ Parity and non-parity memory up to 512MB; supports EDO memory
- ❖ Power management
- ❖ Universal Serial Bus support

Figure 2.7

Intel Triton III VX chipset

❖ PCI bus with ISA support

❖ I/O onboard for up to 4 IDE drives

❖ Pipeline burst cache

❖ Memory access about 10%-15% faster than Triton FX chipset

❖ Parity and non-parity memory up to 512MB; supports EDO memory; supports synchronous DRAM

Figure 2.8

❖ Power management

❖ Universal Serial Bus support

Opti Viper chipset

❖ PCI bus and VL bus with ISA support

❖ I/O onboard

❖ Up to 2MB of write-back pipeline burst cache

❖ Parity and non-parity memory up to 512MB; supports EDO memory

SIS chipset

❖ PCI bus and VL bus

❖ I/O onboard for up to 4 IDE devices

❖ Pipeline burst cache

❖ 2MB of write-back cache

❖ Parity and non-parity memory up to 512MB; supports EDO memory

Figure 2.9

❖ Power management

We have just seen how selecting a chipset eliminates many of the decisions that we have to make in selecting a motherboard. However, there are a few other things to consider. You should select a motherboard that has a BIOS from one of the major manufacturers. The BIOS is a small chip which contains the most important program instructions for initializing and testing the computer at startup, setting the Plug 'n' Play devices and handling the computer's basic functions for inputting and outputting data, for example. We recommend a motherboard which has a Plug 'n Play *Flash BIOS*. A flash BIOS is made using a chip that is reprogrammable, meaning that the functions can be easily updated at a later time using a program supplied by the manufacturer. The program is usually supplied on a diskette when you buy the motherboard. The major BIOS manufacturers are AMI (American Megatrends International), Award, DTK and Microid Research and Phoenix.

Plug 'n' Play

This is a relatively new standard whose goal is to automate the configuration of new peripherals in a computer system. When the BIOS and operating system recognize a new Plug 'n' Play peripheral, it can automatically decide how to configure the IRQs, DMAs, and other technical specifications. Plug 'n Play requires that the BIOS, operating system and peripheral device all meet the Plug 'n Play specifications.

Select a motherboard that has a built-in mouse port. If your motherboard doesn't have a mouse port, then to add a mouse to your computer system, you'll either have to use one of the computer's two serial ports or buy a separate add-on card for a mouse.

A built-in game port is another convenient feature to look for. But don't be too critical if the motherboard doesn't have a built-in game port; most sound cards also have a game port and since you'll probably want a sound card in your PC, you'll also get a game port at the same time.

Some motherboards are better laid out than others. For example, we've found motherboards that are unable to use a full-length add-on card because it won't fit into the slot without interfering with one or more other components on the motherboard. Check the layout to assure yourself that this won't be a problem.

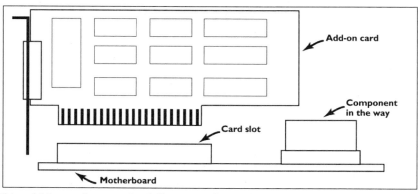

Figure 2.10 This add-in card cannot be fully inserted into the slot because the component already on the motherboard is in the way

To make their products more attractive, some manufacturers have added other features to their motherboards:

❖ Built-in video display card

❖ Built-in sound card

❖ Built-in SCSI I/O adapter

In order to build a flexible system, we recommend that you select a motherboard that does not have any of these additional features. While the price of a motherboard with a built-in video display card, or sound card may be attractive, you loose the some of the flexibility in future upgrades. Instead, we recommend separate plug-in cards that perform one of these particular function. By taking this approach, you'll build a system that can be easily upgraded at a later time.

Special Tip

Don't buy a motherboard without the user's manual. The user's manual has very specific and necessary instructions for setting the various jumpers and switches. Configuring your motherboard is is one of the most critical steps in building a trouble-free PC and the user's manual is a required part.

Cases And Power Supplies

Selecting a case and power supply is mostly a choice of deciding which of the two major styles of case you prefer. These two styles are *desktop* and *tower*. In simplest terms, cases vary by their size, profile, and color.

As its name suggests, a desktop computer cases is meant to sit on top of a desk - horizontally. A desktop case is designed so that it doesn't take up a lot of space on the desk. The tradeoff of using this more compact desktop case is that there usually isn't a lot of room inside the case to add a lot of peripherals.

Figure 2.11 A desktop case

Tower cases are meant to stand upright either on the floor or on a shelf. There are variations to the tower cases. You'll often find a full tower, a midi-tower and a mini-tower case according to the height of the unit. As you'd expect, the larger the case, the more space there is inside the case for adding components. If you're planning to build a PC with four hard drives, two floppies and lots of add-ons, you should probably buy a full tower case.

Whether you buy a desktop or a tower, the case most likely includes the power supply. The power supply produces a regulated source of electricity - meaning that the voltage doesn't vary. Power supplies have electrical connectors that supply the motherboard and other devices with +5V, -5V and + 12V. A power supply is rated by the number of watts of power which they can deliver to all connected devices. Earlier computers could easily use up to 200 watts of power. But the components used by today's computers are much more energy efficient and we haven't seen a computer in a long time that's required more than 200 watts of power. Most power supplies are rated for 230 watts or more so there's a safety margin in the event you need a little extra power.

Figure 2.12 A tower case

Most tower cases and some desktop cases also include a cooling fan. This fan removes the heat from within the enclosed case. Excessive heat can cause premature failure of the components. Pentium CPUs generate considerably more heat than their 486 predecessors. While you may not like its continuous hum, it's a good idea to choose a case - desktop or tower - that has a cooling fan.

Besides the power connectors, there are several other connectors that will be attached to various components in the computer. These may include connectors for the power indicator, turbo switch, hard drive LED and built-in speaker.

Make sure that the case you select also includes a small box or plastic bag containing the mounting and accessory hardware. These include various size screws, washers, brackets and standoffs that are essential to assembling your computer.

Memory

A computer's main memory or RAM is built from small circuit boards called SIMMs. Pentium motherboards are designed to use standard 72-pin SIMMs. If you count the "fingers" on the bottom edge of a SIMM, you'll see why it is called a 72-pin module.

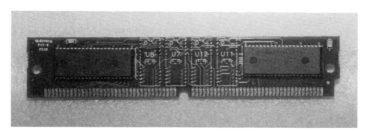

Figure 2.13 A 72-pin SIMM

Most Pentium motherboards have four 72-pin sockets. The four sockets are organized as two banks of two sockets each. These are identified as Bank 0 and Bank 1. By design, both sockets in a bank must contain SIMMs; therefore you must add SIMMs to the motherboard in pairs; you cannot add a single SIMM at a time. Bank 0 must be filled before Bank 1. For a 16MB system, you can use two 8MB SIMMs in Bank 0 or four 4MB SIMMs in both Bank 0 and Bank 1.

Figure 2.14 This motherboard has four 72-pin SIMM sockets

When you're buying memory, you may see it advertised with a lot of technical numbers. Here's an example of an advertisement for memory:

4MB 1x32 70ns 72-pin SIMMs	$35
8MB 2x32 60ns 72-pin SIMMs w/EDO	$60
16MB 4x36 70ns 72-pin SIMMs w/parity	$100
32MB 8x32 60ns 72-pin SIMMs	$220

Figure 2.15 Here's a sample of how you might see memory advertised

To help you understand what this all means, let's decode some of this jargon. When you select RAM, you have to specify several characteristics:

❖ **Amount of memory on the SIMM**
Represents the amount of RAM that the module adds to your computer. The amount is stated in MB (for millions of bytes).

❖ **Arrangement of chips on the SIMM**

Describes the way in which the individual chips are accessed on the SIMM. For our purposes, you can consider this value to be another way of describing the amount of memory on the SIMM listed in the table on the right.

Table 2.16	
Arrangement	Capacity
1X32 or 1X36	4MB
2X32 or 2X36	8MB
4X32 or 4X36	16MB
8X32 or 8X36	32MB

❖ **Time to access data**

Represents the amount of time required to access any piece of data within the SIMM. The time is represented in ns (for *nanoseconds* which is one-billionth of a second!!!). In the above examples, the 4MB SIMM has a speed of 70 nanoseconds while the 8MB SIMM has a 60 nanosecond speed. For Pentiums 120MHz and above, use 60 nanosecond SIMMs or faster. You can "mix" two SIMMs of different speed, for example 70 ns and 60 ns SIMMs. However, the access speed will be the slower of the pair, 70 ns in this case.

❖ **Parity or non-parity**

Determines whether a SIMM has parity checking. Parity checking is a way to make a computer's memory more reliable. Without parity checking a byte of RAM is composed of 8 bits of memory; with parity checking a byte of RAM is made up of 9 bits of memory. The extra bit is a "check" bit which is used to make sure that the data in the remaining 8 bits is valid. If you see the designation 1x36 or 2x36 or 4x36 or 8x36, then you'll know that this is a SIMM with parity bits. **Note:** Many Pentium motherboards are sold today use non-parity SIMMs. Make sure that the memory you buy matches the type of memory supported by the motherboard. If you are building a PC which absolutely requires the utmost in uptime and data security, choose a motherboard that use parity memory.

❖ **EDO or non-EDO**

EDO stands for Extended Data Out and is a newer type of SIMM that is 10 to 15 percent faster than conventional SIMMs. An EDO SIMM fits in all motherboards that accept 72-pin SIMMs, but the faster access time is available only if the motherboard is designed specifically to use EDO SIMMs.

Always buy SIMMs in pairs. Most memory specialists recommend that both SIMMs in a pair are made by the same manufacturer. For the small difference in price between EDO and non-EDO SIMMs, we recommend that you go with the EDO type and enjoy the performance gain. A 16MB system is the minimum that we recommend to take advantage of the Pentium's power, especially if you're planning to run Windows 95. You can try to get away with 8MB, but we don't think you'll be happy with an under performing PC.

Cache Memory

There isn't much to selecting cache memory. When you're selecting your motherboard, the salesman will most likely ask you if you also want to add cache memory. Depending on the design of the motherboard, you'll want to add one of two types of cache memory: static RAM chips or COAST modules (some motherboards such as ours has onboard cache built-in, but also lets us upgrade to more cache memory by adding a COAST module).

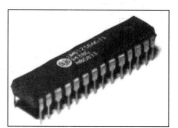

Figure 2.17 Static RAM cache

The figure on the right shows a single SRAM chip. SRAM is the abbreviation for <u>S</u>tatic <u>RAM</u>. These chips come in different capacities. If your motherboard has 8 sockets totaling 256K, you'll want to buy eight 32K X 8 SRAM chips which costs roughly $40. Here's some ballpark prices for SRAM:

- ❖ 32K X 8 SRAM $5.00 each

- ❖ 64K X 8 SRAM $8.50 each

- ❖ 128K X 8 SRAM $16.00 each

A second type of add-on cache is supplied as a COAST module as we see in the figure on the right. This module easily plugs into a special socket on the motherboard. If your motherboard has a slot for a COAST cache module, you'll be able to buy a 256K module for about $40.

Cache memory is very fast, with cycle times of about 15 nanoseconds. By adding cache to your system, you can enhance the performance of your computer system for a very nominal cost. In general, cache memory is a good investment for your computer.

Figure 2.18 A typical COAST module

Video Display Cards

Selecting a good video display card is critical to making your PC perform well. Pentiums are so powerful and the amount of data that these CPUs can process is considerable. Most of you will use either Windows 3.11 and Window 95. These graphical interfaces "draw" tremendous amounts of text to the screen by way of the video display card. Thus a slow video display card can *waste* the speed of a fast Pentium CPU.

Earlier PCs were designed around the classic 16-bit ISA (Industry Standard Association) bus or the later 32-bit EISA (Extended ISA) bus. This limited pathway to the video card was therefore a bottleneck to fast video performance. If you're thinking about using an older ISA-bus video display card, DON'T. Today's newer VL-bus or PCI video display cards offer a tremendous performance gain over the ISA video display cards.

The VL-Bus (VESA Local bus) was designed to improve the video performance of ISA systems, by moving data between the CPU and the video display card at a much faster speed. Today, both the PCI and VLB system bus on a Pentium motherboard provides a wider, streamlined pathway for the video data which greatly improves the overall PC performance. Don't try to save money by buying an older generation video display card. Instead, buy a PCI or VLB video display card (matching the system bus of your motherboard).

We'll repeat some earlier advice again. The PCI bus is now the de facto standard for Pentiums. We recommend a PCI motherboard and video display card.

In selecting a video display card, you usually have to select the type and amount of memory for the card. These two factors determine the display speed and maximum display resolution of the card. There are two types of memory - DRAM and VRAM. DRAM is the same type of memory as the computer system's main memory. A card with DRAM is less expensive to buy than the same card with VRAM. A video display card with VRAM can generate the display faster. VRAM is "dual-ported" - there are two paths to the same memory location. This second path lets the video circuitry access the VRAM at the same time as the CPU so that neither one has to wait for the other.

Figure 2.19 A PCI video display card

A video display card with more memory can operate at a higher resolution. If you're planning to run mostly word processing or accounting applications on your PC, then 1MB of video memory is probably sufficient. But more highly graphical applications such as CAD, games or desktop publishing, you may want to consider a card with 2MB of video memory. Keep in mind that the maximum resolution of the card can be achieved only if your monitor is capable of displaying that resolution. At a later point in time, you can upgrade a 1MB DRAM video card for about $40-$50 to gain higher resolution and color depth.

Well known manufacturers of video display cards include the following:

- ❖ ATI
- ❖ Cirrus Logic
- ❖ Diamond
- ❖ Genoa
- ❖ Hercules
- ❖ Matrox
- ❖ Number Nine
- ❖ Orchid
- ❖ Trident

Monitors

In selecting a monitor, remember that not all monitors are created equal. The major factors to consider are the screen size, dot pitch, refresh rate, interlace, maximum resolution and energy saving features.

The most economical monitors are 14" in size. If you spend a lot of time (two or more hours a day) using the computer, you'll appreciate a 15" or 17" monitor. Some users such as graphic artists and CAD users may even want to a consider 21" monitor even though one will cost you a leg and an arm. But a larger screen is certainly easier on the eyes.

The characters and graphics on a color monitor are formed by a set of three color *triads*. The dot pitch is a measure of the spacing between adjacent triads. When this measure is smaller, the characters and graphics appear tighter" or sharper to the eye. Less expensive monitors have a dot pitch of .35 or .38 mm . We recommend a monitor with a dot pitch of .28 mm or smaller. Some of the more expensive monitors have a dot pitch of .25 mm.

The refresh rate is the frequency at which the characters and graphics are redrawn on the screen. The higher the frequency, the less the image appears to flicker. For flicker-free viewing, the refresh rate should be about 70 Hz or 70 times a second. Almost all monitors today are have a multisync feature. This means that they are able to adjust their refresh rate within a range of values to match the signals that the video display card outputs to the monitor.

A monitor redraws the screen by using an electron gun which shoots a beam at inside of the screen from the left side to the right in lines starting at the top to the bottom. A monitor is designed to operate in one of two ways: interlace or non-interlace mode. In non-interlace mode, the screen is painted from top to bottom by an electron beam in a single pass. Monitors that operate in interlace mode, paint the screen in two passes; during the first pass the odd number lines are redrawn and while the even numbers are redrawn during the second pass. In either mode, the time to redraw the entire screen is identical. However, less expensive monitors use interlace mode since they can be designed to operate at lower refresh rates. Non-interlace monitors appear to have a more stable image, but may cost a bit more. For highest quality, choose a non-interlace monitor.

The maximum resolution is the number of individually addressable pixels that the monitor is capable of displaying. We recommend that you select a monitor that has a resolution of at least 1024 x 768 pixels. Many monitors can display up to 1280 x 1024 pixels, but they may cost more. Keep in mind that the a monitor's maximum resolution cannot be achieved unless the video display card is capable of operating at that resolution as well.

A monitor is one of the heaviest consumers of electrical power. Newer energy saving monitors are capable of going to "sleep" when the computer is sitting idle for a length of time. A computer's video display card must send and the monitor must be capable of responding to a DPMS (Display Power Management Signal). Selecting an energy saving monitor can save from $25 to $75 a year in electrical costs.

Some of the brand names in monitors include the following:

| ❖ Acer | ❖ Hitachi | ❖ NEC | ❖ Princeton |
| ❖ Samtron | ❖ Sony | ❖ Viewsonic | ❖ Zenith |

CPU Cooling Fan

A Pentium CPU has in the neighborhood of 3 million transistors jam packed into a package about 2" x 2" in size. Talk about crowded! All of those busy electrons racing around inside a small ceramic square create a lot of heat. A Pentium uses about 15 watts of energy, so we strongly recommend that you use a cooling fan to remove the heat from the CPU.

A cooling fan is actually made of two parts: the heat sink and the fan. The heat sink is a square metal plate that sits on top of the Pentium. The fan housing clips over the top of the metal plate and locks the assembly in place. The connectors on the fan are then connected to either a motherboard connector or a power supply connector.

Figure 2.20 This CPU cooling fan will keep the Pentium running cool

Although this book is about building a Pentium computer, the new Cyrix 6x86 CPUs are plug compatible with the Pentiums. We expect that some computer builders may choose to use these very capable and competitively priced CPUs on their motherboards.

> **Special Tip**
>
> Do yourself a favor...don't run a Pentium CPU without a cooling fan.

Another word of caution: the Cyrix CPUs require about 22 watts of power and therefore generate significantly more heat than a Pentium. If you install a Cyrix CPU, make sure that you install a quality CPU cooling fan.

I/O Card

I/O is a symbol which stands for Input / Output. An I/O card provides the primary input and output connections for the CPU.

If you selected a motherboard that doesn't have onboard I/O, then you'll have to buy a separate I/O card. An I/O card is a low cost add-in card that plugs into one of the add-on slots. In particular, we're interested in an IDE I/O card, not a SCSI I/O card. The IDE (for Integrated Drive Electronics) I/O card was originally designed to connect up to two low cost hard drives to the computer. Along the way, IDE became so popular that tape backup and CD-ROM drives were designed to use this inexpensive way to connect to the computer. Now the newer EIDE (Enhanced IDE) interface allows for faster data transfer and connections for up to four IDE devices (hard drives, tape drives, CD-ROM drives, etc.).

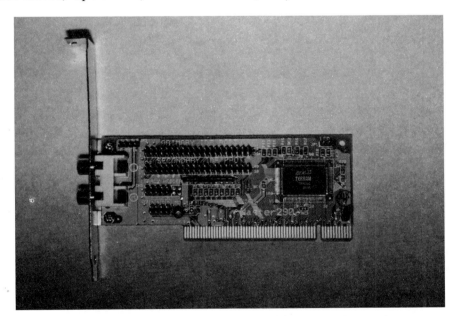

Figure 2.21 If your motherboard does not have built-in I/O, then you'll have to buy a separate I/O card similar to this one; it fits into a PCI slot

When you're shopping for an I/O card, select one which supports the EIDE standard so that the devices that you connect to it can take advantage of the higher data transfer rate. Most EIDE I/O cards will support up to four fixed drives (hard drives and CD-ROM drives).

The I/O card also has connections for other types of input and output devices. Almost all I/O cards will support the following:

- ❖ Two floppy disk drives
- ❖ Two serial (communication) ports
- ❖ One parallel port
- ❖ One game port

Be sure to select an I/O card whose serial port is 16550 UART compatible. This ensures that the serial port is capable of communicating at higher data transfer rates without "losing" data - in other words, making it more reliable.

Keyboard

Many different keyboards are available but they all fall into one of two categories: standard and ergonomic designs. The older style keyboard has 84-keys and we doubt that you'll find these for sale any more. The extended AT-style keyboard has 101-keys including a numeric keypad and a second set of cursor keys. A new Windows 95 keyboard has two additional keys.

Figure 2.22   Standard and ergonomic style keyboards

Ergonomic keyboards are shaped differently. They are designed to fit the contour of your hands are said to be easier on your wrists and fingers. Figure 2.22 shows a standard and ergonomic style keyboard.

If you type a lot, you should consider an ergonomic style keyboard. For example, the Microsoft Natural keyboard positions the hands slightly apart from one another. It takes a short time to get used to touch typing in this position, but it is quite comfortable to use.

The major suppliers of keyboards include the following:

❖ Acer	❖ Alps	❖ BTC
❖ Cherry	❖ Chicony	❖ Focus
❖ Fujitsu	❖ Keytronix	❖ Microsoft
❖ Mitsumi	❖ Qtronix	❖ Reveal

Mouse

We've lumped mice and trackballs and touchpads into the mouse category. These devices are all used to move the mouse pointer around on the screen.

One advantage of trackballs and touchpads over mice is that they don't require a large surface area in which to operate.

Here's a few of the popular "mouse" devices:

Figure 2.23 Mice and trackballs and touchpads let you move the mouse pointer around on the screen

These devices are made by companies such as: Alps, Genius, Logitech, Microsoft and Mitsumi.

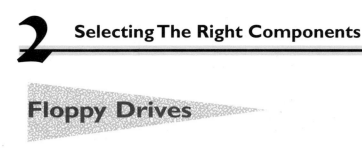

Floppy Drives

Floppy drives are for either 5.25" or 3.5" diskettes. Just a few short years ago, almost all commercial software was distributed on the 5.25" diskette size. Now, very little software is made for the 5.25" format. Buy a 5.25" only if you have a need to transfer files between computers which still use these antiquated drives.

A lot of commercial software is still distributed on 3.5" diskette so you'll want a 3.5" floppy drive. You can buy a brand name 3.5" drive such as Alps, Mitsumi, Panasonic, Sony and Teac for $25 to $60.

Hard Drives

There's a common saying that "you can never have too much hard disk space". It was true years ago and it's just as true today. Years ago, hard drive space was "hardly" affordable. But today you can hardly afford to do without gobs of space. Prices for IDE hard drives are so attractive that you shouldn't buy a hard drive with less than 1 GB capacity. In fact, the price difference between a 1 GB hard drive and a 1.6 GB or 2 GB drive is very small, so we recommend that you select one with a larger capacity for your system.

Access time used to be a big consideration, but most drives deliver a track-to-track seek time of under 12 milliseconds, which is excellent. Don't worry too much about two or three millisecond difference.

Select a drive from a major manufacturer:

- ❖ Conner
- ❖ Fujitsu
- ❖ IBM
- ❖ Maxstor
- ❖ Microsoft
- ❖ NEC
- ❖ Quantum
- ❖ Samsung
- ❖ Seagate
- ❖ Toshiba
- ❖ Western Digital

CD-ROM Drives

You'll be able to find great bargains on 4X and slower CD-ROM drives. Resist the temptation and buy a 6X or 8X CD-ROM drive instead. Since you're building a fast Pentium computer system, you won't want to be slowed down by an older CD-ROM drive, especially if you plan to use your system for CD-ROM video applications.

CD-ROM drives can be connected to your computer in one of three ways: through the IDE interface, through a SCSI interface or through a proprietary interface. To minimize complexity, choose an IDE CD-ROM drive. We selected an IDE CD-ROM drive for the computer illustrated in this book. This eliminates the need for a separate add-in card to support the CD-ROM drive.

Again, select a drive from a major manufacturer:

- Acer
- Creative Labs
- Gold Star
- Hitachi
- Mitsumi
- NEC
- Pioneer
- Reveal
- Samsung
- Sanyo
- Sony
- Teac
- Toshiba

Sound Cards

There are many different varieties of sound cards. Almost all sound cards are "Sound Blaster" compatible meaning that programs written to work with Sound Blaster cards will also work with these sound card as well.

We're not sound card experts, but we can definitely hear the difference in quality between a conventional 8-bit sound card and a newer wave table sound card. If you're on a tight budget, buy a 16-bit "Sound Blaster compatible" sound card. If you feel rich, buy one of the new 32-bit wave table sound cards. We recommend that you look for a sound card that is Plug 'n Play compatible which greatly simplifies setup and configuration. For the computer in this book, we selected a 16-bit Plug 'n Play sound card.

The major makers of sound cards are:

- Creative Labs
- Gravis
- Media Vision
- Reveal
- Turtle Beach

Modems

Are you planning to access the Internet by modem? If you've ever viewed a Web page at 9600 or 14,400 BPS, then you'll know why you shouldn't buy one of these slower modems. They'll keep you waiting and staring at the monitor forever. Do yourself a favor and select a modem that's at least 28.8 KBPS.

Some metropolitan areas now provide ISDN service. Using ISDN, you can connect to many service providers at speeds up to 128 KBPS! An ISDN modem is more expensive than a conventional modem, but if you are working from home or are going to be transferring large amounts of data, an investment in the more expensive ISDN modem will make your work more practical. Some ISDN modems are "combos" - they are backward compatible with conventional analog modems and also provide the faster digital technology of ISDN lines.

Well-know makers of modems include: Boca, Cardinal, Hayes, Motorola, Practical Peripherals, Supra, U.S. Robotics and Zoom.

Speakers

If you're familiar with hi fi music speakers for your home stereo system, then you know that you can spend anywhere between $10 and $2000 for a speaker. It's almost the same for computer speakers. Computer speakers differ from conventional speakers in that they are self-amplified.

The inexpensive speakers are battery powered. We don't recommend them, since you'll surely spend a lot of money for batteries.

Most computer speakers are AC powered and have separate volume and tone controls.

You'll probably choose your speakers based on the maximum volume that you need from your multimedia programs and games.

Leading speaker manufacturers are:

❖ Altec-Lansing	❖ Bose	❖ Inland
❖ JBL	❖ Koss	❖ Labtec
❖ Reveal	❖ Sony	❖ Yamaha

Tape Backup

With today's large hard drive capacity, it's not practical to back up your valuable data to floppy diskette like it was a short time ago. Many of you don't acknowledge the need to back up your data. But there will come a time when you wish you had taken steps to safeguard all of the hours and energy that you spent to make your files, data and programs work perfectly on your system. One day - **POOF** - your hard drive will suddenly die and you'll be left with no way to recover your files.

You can avoid this kind of disaster by investing about $200 to $250 for a tape backup drive and taking regularly scheduled backups.

Some of the more popular tape backup devices are made by Colorado, Conner, Iomega, Syquest and Teac.

Our Shopping List

During the writing of this book, we built two Pentium computers from the ground up. We went shopping on two different occasions and came back with the components listed below. We weren't aggressive shoppers - we didn't try to bargain the prices down.

Although we've listed the prices which we paid for them, the price which you pay for similar items will vary widely depending on where you shop and the trend in computer prices. Currently, there's a downward trend. This means that you'll probably be able to build this same computer for less. But don't take our word for it. Go shopping, ask questions and expect straight answers.

Most of the components for System 1 were brand names. These components were packaged in normal retail shrink wrapped boxes with full manuals and installation diskettes.

For System 2, we tried to buy less expensive components. We bought most of these components at a local computer show. The components were packed "minimally" - usually in a sealed plastic bag with a plain, but clear instruction manual and installation diskettes.

We learned that by careful comparison shopping, we were able to find quality components at excellent prices. It takes some getting used to buying a 2.0 GB hard drive that's wrapped in a plastic bag instead of a 4-color, factory wrapped box. You'll have to decide if you need the security of full retail packaging or would rather save your hard earned dollars buying "bulk" packaged components.

System 1	
Intel Pentium 166MHz CPU	$250 installed
P55-TH PCI-ISA motherboard w/Triton II chipset, I/O onboard with mouse port handles up to 200 MHz CPUs	$165 boxed
2 - 8MB 2 x 32 60ns 72-pin EDO SIMMS	$120 bagged
Number 9 9FX Motion 531 PCI video card 1MB DRAM	$105 boxed
Acer 6X E-IDE/ATAPI CD-ROM drive	$85 boxed
Maxstor 72004AP/A 2.0 GB hard drive	$260 bagged
AGI LS-808D Mini Tower Case	$55 boxed
Panasonic 3.5" 1.44MB floppy drive	$35 boxed
Focus Windows 95 keyboard	$22 boxed
Microsoft PS/2 style mouse	$35 boxed
Coolder Master CPU cooling fan	$12 boxed
Creative Labs SB16 Plug n Play sound card	$90 boxed
Sun-690H stereo speakers	$25 boxed

System 2	
Intel Pentium 166MHz CPU	$250 installed
P51437/250A motherboard w/Triton chipset, I/O onboard with mouse port handles up to 200MHz CPUs	$120 boxed
2 - 8MB 2 x 32 60ns 72-pin EDO SIMMS	$120 bagged
Trident PCI video card 1MB DRAM	$85 bagged
Mitsumi FX 600 6X E-IDE/ATAPI CD-ROM drive	$69 bagged
Maxstor 72004AP/A 2.1 GB hard drive	$250 bagged
Generic PC-F31 Mini Tower Case 230 watt power supply	$48 boxed
Mitsumi 3.5" 1.44MB floppy drive	$22 bagged
Mitsumi Windows 95 keyboard	$13 bagged
Generic PS/2 style mouse	$9 bagged
Super Cooler CPU cooling fan	$10 boxed
Creative Labs SB16 Plug n Play sound card	$70 bagged
Inland stereo speakers	$15 bagged

3

Putting Your Computer Together

3 Putting Your Computer Together

Now that you've selected and bought all of your components, you're ready to assemble your computer system. We've laid out a step by step approach that we've successfully used to build and rebuild many different computers. No matter how excited or impatient you are about building your new computer, please follow all of the steps in the order in which we've presented them. We don't want you to make a mistake that ends up "frying" one of the components.

It's easier said than done, but make the effort to clear a flat, work area about six foot by four foot in size so that you can assemble your PC without falling all over yourself.

An oversized card table or an unused workbench or desk works well. The work surface should be clean. If the work surface cannot be washed, spread clean, white paper over the area. We don't recommend using newspaper because it's hard to find small parts when they drop on news articles and pictures.

The work area should be well lighted; it's usually dark when you're working inside a computer case and the extra light will make assembling your PC much easier. Stay away from drafty areas since small parts are likely to be blown away and lost.

Figure 3.1 A clear well-lighted work area speeds the assembly

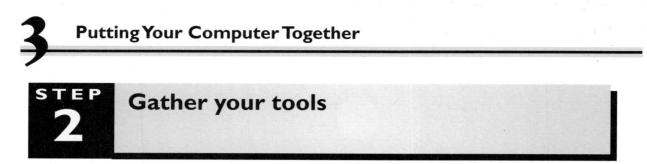

STEP 2 Gather your tools

Contrary to what you might think, you don't need very many tools to assemble a computer. Most of you will have the necessary tools already. Here's what you'll need:

- ❖ Phillips Screwdriver #1 head

- ❖ Screwdriver 1/8" blade

- ❖ Nutdriver 3/8"

- ❖ Long-nose pliers

- ❖ Several small paper cups (the small bathroom size Dixie cups are great) for holding small screws and parts

- ❖ Large mouse pad or small hand towel on which to place the motherboard

- ❖ A pen and a pad of paper to take notes

- ❖ Hammer - to be used only when you can't get the computer to work <u>JUST KIDDING</u>!

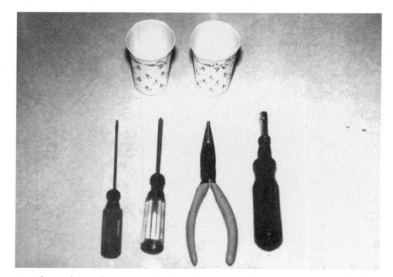

Figure 3.2   These were the only tools we used to build our PC (although we really didn't need the hammer)

If the only Phillips head screwdriver you own is too big or too small, then STOP. Go to a hardware store and buy one that's the correct size. You risk damaging the components or stripping the screw heads by using the wrong tool. A new tool costs only a few dollars. Compare this small expense to the amount of money that you've invested in your new computer.

Prepare the case

Remove the case from its packaging and place it upright on your work surface with the back of the case facing you. Remove the case's cover. Usually five or six hex head screws are used to attach the cover to the frame. Unscrew these and place them in a small paper cup. Label the cup so that you'll know where the screws came from. You can set the cover aside and away from the work area for now. You won't need the cover for a while.

Figure 3.3 Removing the screws from the back of the case

Now lay the case horizontally with the motherboard chassis closest to the work surface and the power supply closest to you as in Figure 3.4.

Figure 3.4 Position the case with the back facing towards you

Some cases, especially tower models, have a removable cage in which you can mount some of the storage devices - floppies, hard drives, CD-ROMs, tape backup drives, etc. After you remove the cage by unscrewing a few hex head screws as in Figure 3.5, you'll have an less obstructed work area inside the case.

Figure 3.5 Remove the cage from the case

After the cage is removed, the entire chassis on bottom of the case is exposed as in Figure 3.6. This makes is much easier for you to mount the motherboard in the case.

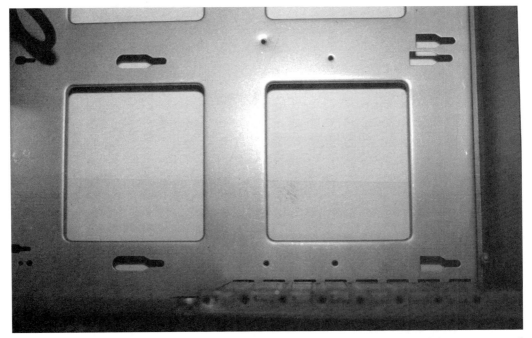

Figure 3.6 Plastic standoffs are later inserted into the oblong cutouts in the chassis to mount the motherboard to the case

Note the oblong cutouts in the chassis. In a few minutes, you'll see how the plastic standoffs are inserted in these cutouts to mount the motherboard to the case (See Step 9).

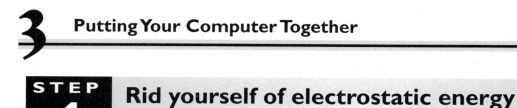

STEP 4 — Rid yourself of electrostatic energy

Electrostatic energy (we used to call it static electricity) is capable of damaging computer circuits in some of the components. To prevent damaging them, you'll need to discharge yourself of this deadly "disease" before handling the components.

A simple way to do this is to ground yourself. When your power supply is plugged into a three-prong wall outlet, the computer case is also grounded. To discharge yourself of the electrostatic energy, touch the metal computer case.

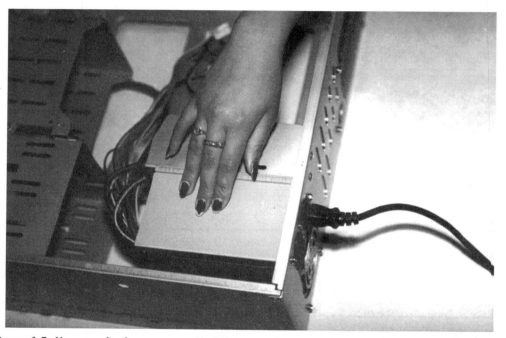

Figure 3.7 You can discharge yourself of electrostatic energy by grounding yourself to the case

Another way to discharge yourself of electrostatic energy is to wear a wrist strap. This device is like a watch with a leash. The leash is connected to a ground and the other end wraps around your wrist. By wearing the wrist strap, you're always grounded.

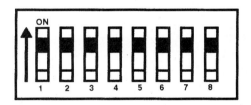

STEP 5 Configure the motherboard

The next step is to *configure* or set up the motherboard. You'll now have to <u>carefully read the user's manual</u> for your motherboard. You'll have to find the instructions for setting any DIP switches and/or jumpers for the computer that you are about to build. Before you get started, we'll cover a few basics that will be helpful.

DIP switches are usually found in sets of from two to eight miniature light switches on a small plastic base which is soldered to the top of the motherboard. The individual switches are numbered and the label on the plastic base indicates whether a given switch is on or off. To turn a switch on, use a ball-point pen to move the switch in the **ON** direction. To turn a switch off, move the switch **opposite the ON** direction. A row of DIP switches on a motherboard looks like this:

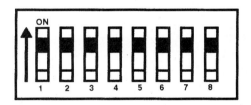

Figure 3.8 A DIP switch that might be found on a motherboard

A jumper is another kind of switch. You'll notice that there are several metal pins sticking up from the surface of the motherboard. The pins are labeled JP1 or J10, for example. A jumper cap is a small metal connector surrounded by insulated plastic (most jumper caps are black in color). When you put the jumper cap on two of the pins, you *close* or *turn on* the switch. If you don't put a jumper cap on the pins, then the switch is *open* or *turned off*. In some cases the pins on the motherboard are paired and labeled 1 and 2; in other cases, there may be three pins labeled 1, 2 and 3. You may be asked to select one option by jumpering pins 1 and 2 or other option by jumpering pins 2 and 3.

In Figure 3.9, the setting is made by jumpering pins 2 and 3.

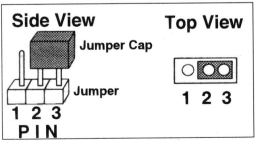

Figure 3.9 A typical jumper on a motherboard

In this book we also refer to a *connector*. In one instance, a connector may refer to a set of pins on the motherboard (usually from 2 to 40 pins). A connector may also refer to the black plastic plug at the end of a set of wires or cable which is attached to the pins.

For the Pentium that we're building in this book, we are going configure the motherboard in the following illustration:

Figure 3.10 This Pentium motherboard has a Triton II chipset and built-in I/O board

Here's a schematic diagram of the same motherboard so you can more easily pick out the important landmarks. The labels refer to the jumpers and connectors as they are identified in the Motherboard User's Guide.

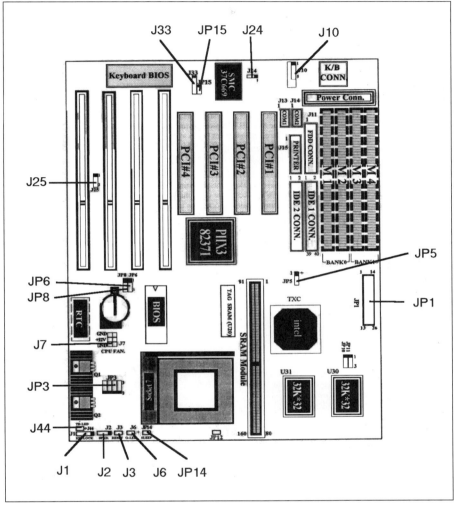

Figure 3.11 Schematic of the Pentium motherboard from Figure 3.10

<u>Before you handle the motherboard, first rid yourself of electrostatic energy.</u>

Place the motherboard on a soft padded surface. A large mouse mat or a terrycloth hand towel will work well. Our motherboard was packed with a white foam pad which is good for preventing any damage to the work surface (the bottom of the motherboard has sharp edges) or to the motherboard itself.

We've reproduced several pages of the user's guide so that you can see what is required to configure this particular motherboard. Unfortunately, most motherboard user's guides are poorly written. The user's guide for this motherboard is no exception. The writer is inconsistent in the way that he labels the jumpers and connectors (he incorrectly uses the notation J and JP which normally signifies connector and jumper respectively). Furthermore, the writer's choice of words, grammar and sentence structure make it more difficult for us to interpret what he's trying to say.

Figure 3.12 is a page from the user's guide that identifies the arrangement of connectors. Since there are no switches or jumpers listed on this page we do not have to set any. We'll use the information on this page again later when completing the motherboard installation.

2-2 Connectors and Jumpers

This section describes all of the connectors and jumpers equipped in the motherboard. Please refer to **Figure 1-1** for actual location of each connector and jumper.

J1   **KeyLock** - Keyboard lock switch & Power LED connector.
      1.Power LED(+)
      2.N/C
      3.GND
      4.Keylock
      5.GND

J2   **Speaker** - connect to the system's speaker for beeping.
      1. Speaker
      2. N/C
      3. GND
      4. GND

J3   **Reset** - Close to restart system.

J44   **Turbo LED indicator** - LED ON when higher speed is selected by a BIOS hot key<CTRL><ALT><+>and also brings system to a slower speed while a hot key<CTRL><ALT><->.

J6   **Power Saving LED indicator(Green-LED)** LED ON when system is in any Saving mode.

J7   **The Power supply of the CPU cooling fan**
      1,2 GND
      3,4 +12v
      5,6 GND

JP5   **IDE LED indicator** - LED ON when Onboard PCI IDE Harddisks activites.

	Interpretation
J1	This is a connector, not a switch. No setting is required
J2	This is a connector, not a switch. No setting is required
J3	This is a connector, not a switch. No setting is required
J44	This is a connector, not a switch. No setting is required
J6	This is a connector, not a switch. No setting is required
J7	This is a connector, not a switch. No setting is required
JP5	This is a connector, not a switch. No setting is required

Figure 3.12 Page 1 of 3 from Motherboard User's Guide

Figure 3.13 is a second page of the user's guide that describes the use of several jumpers. Since we used the factory default settings, we didn't have to change any of the settings listed on this page.

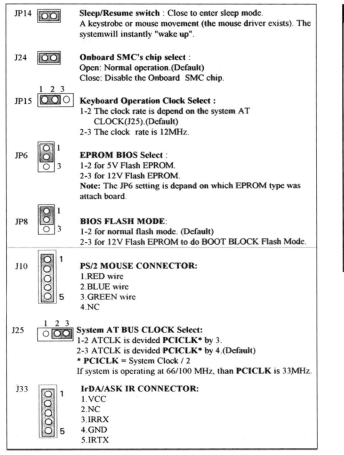

Interpretation	
JP14	Although it is described as a switch, it's actually a connector so no setting is required
J24	The SMC chip select handles the onboard I/O. We'll use the default setting by leaving the jumper OPEN
JP5	We'll use the default setting by leaving pins 1 and 2 jumpered.
JP6	We'll use the default setting by leaving pins 2 and 3 jumpered.
JP8	We'll use the default setting by leaving pins 1 and 2 jumpered.
J10	This is a connector. No setting is required
J25	We'll use the default setting by leaving pins 2 and 3 jumpered.
J33	This is a connector. No setting is required

Figure 3.13 Page 2 of 3 from Motherboard User's Guide

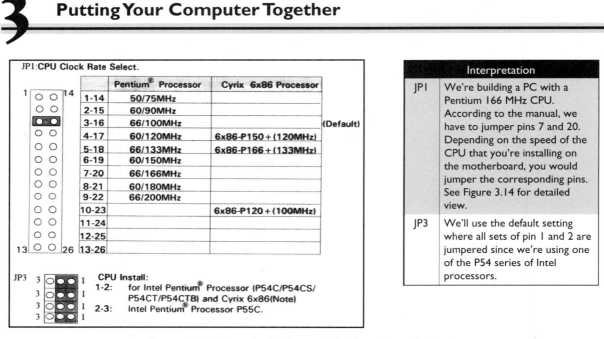

Figure 3.14 Page 3 of 3 from Motherboard User's Guide

Figure 3.15 Jumpering pins 7 and 20 to configure the motherboard for a Pentium P166 CPU

As you can see, there weren't very many jumpers or switches that we needed to set for this particular motherboard. Still, you'll have to read the user's manual for your particular motherboard in detail. If you have questions about the settings, ask the salesperson or technician from whom you bought the motherboard. They have a lot of experience building PCs and should be quite familiar with the specific settings for the motherboards which they sell.

STEP 6 Install the CPU on the motherboard

This is an easy step. All Pentium motherboards have a ZIF socket. ZIF stands for Zero Insertion Force and as its name suggests, you don't have to apply any pressure to insert the CPU into the socket.

Unlatch the small plastic or metal arm on the side of the ZIF socket and lift the arm until it is standing upright. Notice that there is a small notch on one of the four corners of your Pentium CPU. Turn the CPU upside down and you'll see three gold pins that run diagonally to the corner. On the ZIF socket, you'll also see three small holes that run diagonally to the corner. This indicates the alignment of the CPU and

Special Tip
Discharge yourself of any electrostatic energy before you handle the CPU.

socket. You'll only be able to insert the CPU into the socket by aligning the diagonal pins and holes. Carefully insert the CPU into the socket making sure that the CPU is fully seated. You do not have to push the CPU into the socket as it will easily drop into place on its own. If it doesn't, wiggle the arm a bit. See Figures 3.16, 3.17 and 3.18

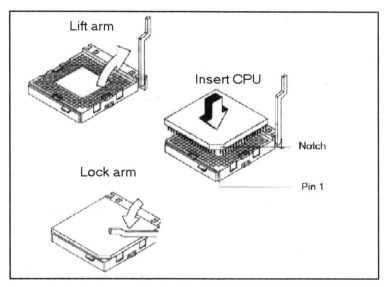

Figure 3.16 Three steps to installing the CPU in the ZIF socket

Figure 3.17 Gently place the CPU into the socket...

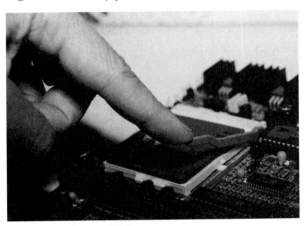

Figure 3.18 ...and lower the arm and lock CPU in place

When the CPU is properly seated in the ZIF socket, lower the arm fully and latch it so that the CPU is locked into place.

STEP 7
Install the cache memory on the motherboard

Some motherboards have cache memory already installed. Figure 3.19 shows a motherboard that was manufactured with 256K of pipeline burst cache onboard.

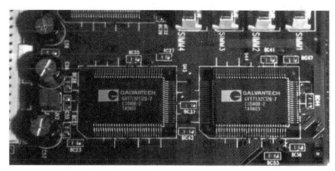

Figure 3.19   Motherboard with onboard cache

Your motherboard may also have onboard cache memory and/ or may have one or more sockets for adding cache memory. The cache memory may be individual static RAM chips or COAST modules.

> **WARNING**
>
> Before you handle the cache memory chips or module, make sure that you've discharged yourself of any electrostatic energy.

If your motherboard uses the individual static RAM chips, then you'll have to install them by aligning the notched corner of the static RAM chip with the notch indicator on the socket and gently pushing the chip into its socket. Be careful not to bend the delicate pins. See Figure 3.20.

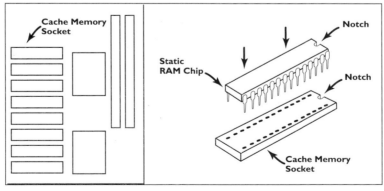

Figure 3.20 Installing static RAM cache

In addition to the onboard cache, this particular motherboard has a socket which accepts a pipeline burst cache (COAST) module. Installing a COAST module, increases the amount of cache memory on this motherboard from 256K to 512K. If you've purchased a COAST module, you can simply plug it into the motherboard. You can only insert the COAST module into its socket in one direction so there's not chance of putting it in backwards. See Figure 3.21

Figure 3.21 Installing a COAST pipeline burst cache module

STEP 8

Install memory on the motherboard

Installing main memory is also easy. Memory is supplied on 72-pin SIMM modules. This motherboard can accept up to four SIMM modules, one in each of the four white sockets in the upper right hand corner of Figure 3.10.

The four sockets are arranged as two banks of two sockets each. In our Motherboard User's Guide, a schematic of the sockets indicated that one is labeled Bank 0 and the other Bank 1. If you are installing only two SIMMs, these must be installed in Bank 0. At a later time, if you want to install two more SIMMs, they'll be installed in Bank 1. Make sure that you know which sockets are Bank 0 and which are Bank 1 as in the following figure:

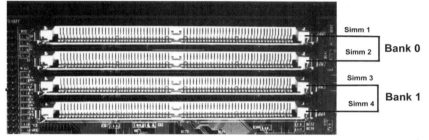

Figure 3.22 Two SIMM sockets each make up Bank 0 and Bank 1

Discharge yourself of electrostatic energy before touching any of the SIMM modules

Pick up one of the SIMM modules. Find the small holes on each side of the module. Beneath one of the holes you'll see a notch. This notch is designed to prevent you from inserting the SIMM module into a socket backwards. Examine the SIMM socket and note which direction you'll have to insert the SIMM module so that the notch will clear the plastic tab. With the metal fingers side down, carefully insert the SIMM module into a socket in Bank 0 in the noted direction. The module in inserted into the socket at a 30 degree angle from vertical. The metal fingers will line up perfectly with the fingers in the socket. If you happen to insert the SIMM backwards, the fingers will not align correctly and the notch will not clear the plastic tab. The holes in the SIMM will align with the pegs on the socket and the metal clips on the sockets will click to indicate that the SIMMs are locked in place. See Figure 3.23 and Figure 3.24.

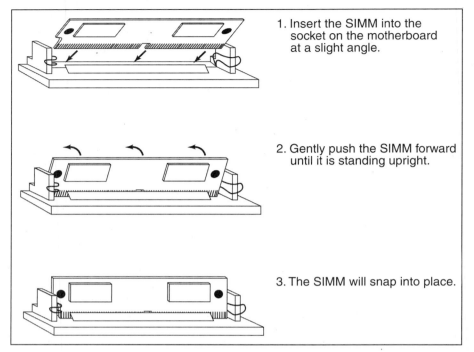

1. Insert the SIMM into the socket on the motherboard at a slight angle.

2. Gently push the SIMM forward until it is standing upright.

3. The SIMM will snap into place.

Figure 3.23 Installing memory on the motherboard

This is what it looks like from a different angle:

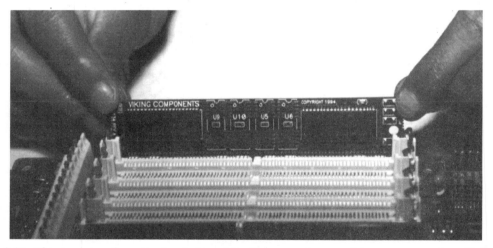

Figure 3.24 This is a view from the front side of the figure on the top of the page as we install the SIMM into a socket

Remember that SIMM modules must be installed in pairs and that both SIMM modules in the same bank must have the same memory capacity. So for example, 16MB of memory is added to a computer system by installing two 8MB SIMMs into one of the banks. Alternatively, you can install four 4MB SIMMs into both of the banks.

STEP 9 Mount the motherboard in the case

Your case includes a small box or plastic bag containing the mounting hardware.

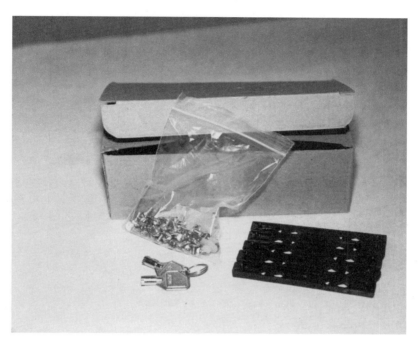

Figure 3.25 A packet containing the hardware for mounting the motherboard to the case

Among the mounting hardware are screws of various sizes and *standoffs*. Here's a picture of several types of standoffs so that you'll be able to identify them.

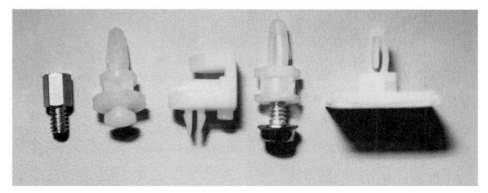

*Figure 3.26 Standoffs - from left to right Brass, Standard, Edge, Screw down, and Adhesive backed
(Courtesy of Skyline Computers, Brookfield, IL)*

As you can see, there are different styles of standoffs. Usually, only the brass, standard and edge standoffs are included with the hardware packet.

A standoff is used to attach the motherboard to the case. At the same time, the standoff holds the motherboard a safe distance away from the metal chassis to prevent unwanted connections from shorting out.

Figure 3.27 Brass standoffs and machine mounting screws.

The brass standoffs in Figure 3.27 are screwed directly into the case. When secured to the brass standoff with a machine screw, the motherboard is grounded to the case.

The trick in mounting the motherboard is to line up the holes in the chassis with the holes in the motherboard. An easy way to do this is to take a large piece of paper, scotch tape it to the bottom of the chassis and carefully trace the outline of the cutouts and small screw holes with a felt marker. Note the location of the keyboard connector cutout on the back side of the case's frame on the paper template. Untape the paper from the chassis. It should look similar to Figure 3.28.

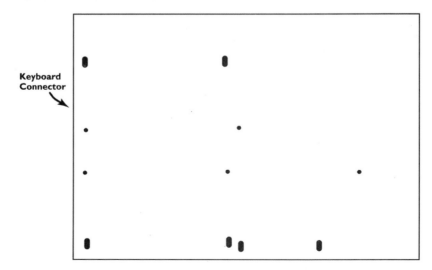

Keyboard Connector

Figure 3.28 This paper template indicates the position of the cutouts and screw holes on the chassis.

Now place the motherboard over the paper template so that the keyboard connector in the same relative position as indicated on the paper template as in Figure 3.29. Move the motherboard until its holes are aligned with the holes that you traced on the template. Not all of the holes will be lined up. Note those holes that <u>are</u> lined up. Draw an 'X' on the paper template to mark the holes that are lined up exactly. These X's are the points at which you will soon attach the motherboard to the chassis. For a secure installation, you'll want to attach the motherboard to the chassis at a minimum of six or seven points.

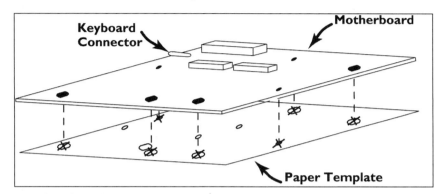

Figure 3.29 Identify the holes on the motherboard which are aligned with the holes in the case.

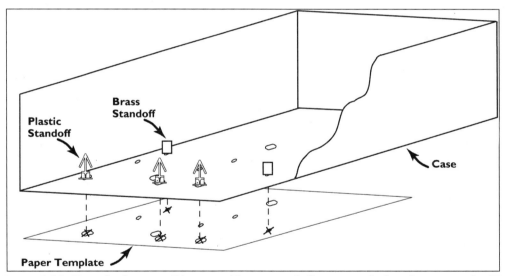

Figure 3.30 X marks the spot. Plastic and brass standoffs are attached to the case at the X's.

Now place the paper template beneath the case once again as in Figure 3.30. The X's on the paper template indicate the points at which the plastic and metal standoffs are attached to the case. Now you'll insert the plastic and metal standoffs in cutouts and holes in the case corresponding to the X's on the paper template.

To attach a plastic standoff to the chassis, insert the short end into the larger end of the oblong cutout and slide it towards the smaller end. Make sure that the sides of the metal opening slide into the plastic groove. See Figure 3.31.

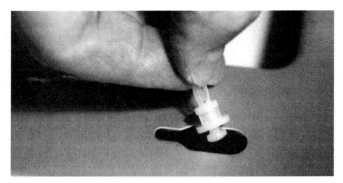

Figure 3.31   Slide the standard plastic standoff into the oblong cutout in the chassis

To attach a metal standoff, simply screw it into the desired chassis holes. The metal standoffs also serve to ground the motherboard to the case.

Attach the desired number of standoffs to the case. Gently lower motherboard into the case and align the holes over the standoffs. First secure the motherboard to the brass standoffs as in the following figure. Screw the motherboard to each of the brass standoffs with the mounting screws from your accessory package. As your doing this, you'll see the heads of the plastic standoffs peeking through the holes in the motherboard as in Figure 3.32. When all of the screws have been secured, gently press the motherboard at a point close to each of the plastic standoffs. The top of the plastic standard standoffs will pop through the holes in the motherboard and open up (like an umbrella) to hold the motherboard in place Tighten the screws again. You've just completed the physical mounting.

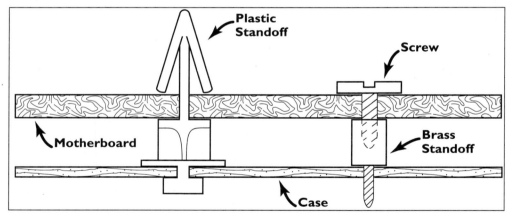

Figure 3.32   This side view shows you how the plastic and brass standoffs are used to mount the motherboard to the chassis

Now check to make sure that there are no surface areas on the bottom of the motherboard that are touching the metal case. If there are, remove the motherboard and reinstall it. Otherwise, the motherboard will short circuit on the case and become damaged. When you're done, the bottom of the case will look similar to Figure 3.33:

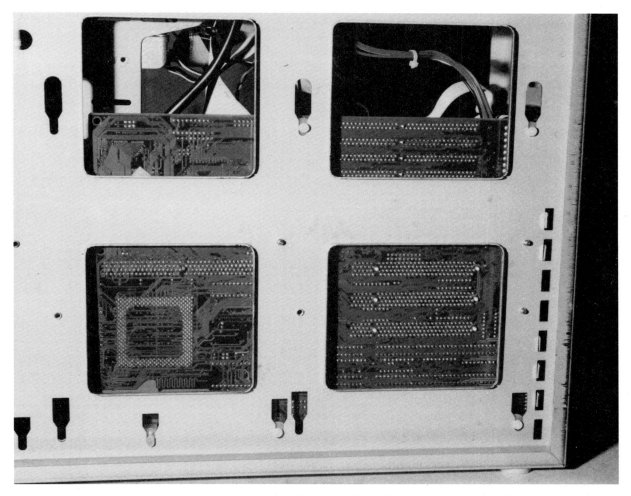

Figure 3.33 A bottom view of the chassis after the motherboard has been mounted to the case using the plastic and brass standoffs

If You Have Trouble

Sometimes the holes in the motherboard just will not line up with the cutouts and screw holes on the chassis.

If this happens, you can purchase either screw down standoffs or adhesive backed standoffs. Either of these standoffs can be placed anywhere on the chassis. For screw down standoffs, you'll have to drill a hole in the desired position on the chassis. For the adhesive backed standoffs, you can remove the protective backing and press the standoff in the desired position.

Connect the power supply to the motherboard

There are usually six or seven sets of wires (harnesses) leading from the power supply. Locate the two connectors, which have six wires each. These connectors are usually labeled P8 and P9. They supply power to the motherboard.

Figure 3.34 shows a power supply that we removed from its case so you could see the connectors more easily.

Figure 3.34   The two sets of wires in the left foreground labeled P8 and P9 have six wires each. These connect to the motherboard.

The connectors are designed to attach to the motherboard in only one direction. If the connector does not attach easily, then it's probably on backwards. The ribbed side of the P8 and P9 connectors should face the power supply connector on the motherboard. Attach both 6-pin connectors (P8 and P9) to the 12-pin connector on the motherboard so that <u>the four black wires are located in the middle</u> of the 12-pin connector. **Check and double-check** to make sure that they're correctly connected so that you won't fry your motherboard.

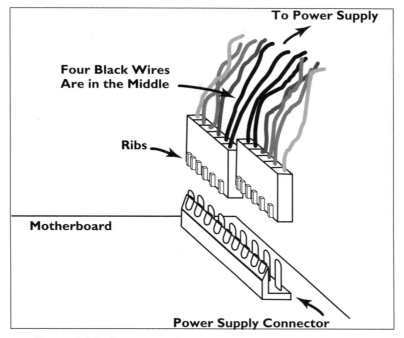

Figure 3.35 Connecting the power supply to the motherboard

Inside the case you'll find several twisted sets of wires leading out from the back of the front panel. The small connectors at the end of the wires are usually clearly labeled to identify their function. These are connected to various pins on the motherboard.

You'll have to consult the motherboard user's manual again to determine the location of the pins to which you'll attach the connectors. Again, using the except pages from the user's guide for our motherboard's users from Figure 3.11, 3.12 and 3.13, we'll walk through these again.

Special Tip

Keep in mind that these connections will likely be different for your case and motherboard. We show you the connections for the motherboard in this example so you can better understand how we were able to determine which connections to make.

❖ **J1 KeyLock**
   Our case has two separate connectors that attach to the pins on connector J1 of this motherboard:

   1. On our case, the green and white wires are for the power LED. This is attached to pins 1, 2 and 3 of J1.

   2. On our case, one of two sets of red and black wires is for the keylock. The other set of red and black wires is for the speaker. Identify the set of wires leading from the keylock and attach this connector to pins 4 and 5 of J1.

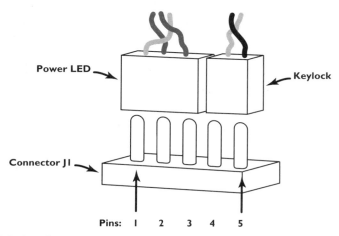

Figure 3.36 Attaching two separate connectors to a 5-pin motherboard connector

❖ **J2 Speaker**

On our case, the second set of black and red wires lead from the speaker. Identify these and attach the connector to pins 1 through 4 of J2.

❖ **J3 Reset**

On our case, the blue and white wires are for the reset switch. Attach the connector to pins 1 and 2 of J3.

❖ **J44 Turbo LED indicator**

On our case, the yellow and white wires are for the turbo LED indicator. Attach the connector to pins 1 and 2 of J44.

❖ **JP5 IDE LED indicator**

On our case, the red and white wires are for the HDD LED. HDD is an abbreviation for <u>H</u>ard <u>D</u>isk <u>D</u>rive which is an IDE device. Attach this connector to pins 1 and 2 of JP5.

Figure 3.37 Most of the "other" connectors are on the edge of the motherboard closest to the front on the case

STEP 12 Install the CPU cooling fan

The Pentium generates a lot of heat. You'll have to install a CPU cooling fan to prevent it from overheating and causing damage to itself.

A CPU cooling fan consists a metal heat sink and the fan housing. Before installing the cooling fan, first make sure that the top of the CPU is clean and free from dirt and grit. If not, gently wipe the top ceramic surface with a cloth. To work properly, the heat sink has to make good contact with the top surface of the CPU. Fit the heat sink carefully over the top of the CPU. Next clip the fan housing over both the heat sink and the CPU making sure that it is securely fastened to the edge of the ZIF socket. Most fan housings clasp over the edge of the socket.

Figure 3.38 Installing the CPU cooling fan

Plug the cooling fan cable into a power supply connector. Make sure that the other wires or cables will not obstruct the airflow of the fan.

Pause: Tips For Installing Add-on Cards

Before we continue, we want to take a short break to explain how to install add-on cards in the expansion slots on the motherboard. In some computer cases, the expansion slot covers are stamped into the case's back panel.. To remove a slot cover, carefully bend it back and forth until the bottom "tears" away from the panel. As you do this, be careful not to damage any of the tiny components on the motherboard. Figure 3.38 below shows how you remove one of the expansion slot covers.

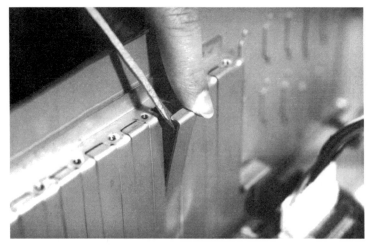

Figure 3.39   Removing an expansion slot cover from the back panel of the case

In other computer cases, the expansion slot covers are screwed into the back panel. To remove a slot cover, unscrew the screw holding the cover in place.

Here's some tips that you should follow when installing any card into an expansion slot:

Tips
Here's a couple of tips that you should follow when installing any card into an expansion slot:
❖ Carefully insert the edge of the card into the slot
❖ Rock the board back and forth slightly from front to back until it seats securely in the slot and the metal fingers are making positive contact
❖ Check that no part of the card is pressing on any of the delicate motherboard components underneath
❖ Verify that the metal plate on the card aligns perfectly with the back of the case
❖ Screw the metal plate into the case to complete the physical installation.

Now we're ready to connect the peripherals. This motherboard has built-in onboard I/O. You may have bought a separate I/O card. If so, you can insert it into one of the ISA slots on the motherboard and secure it with a screw to the back of the case. In subsequent steps, when we refer to "connectors on the motherboard", you should substitute "connectors on the I/O board".

If you've removed the cage, you can now reinstall it since the motherboard is securely seated in the case.

Here's the cables that are used to attach the peripherals to the motherboard:

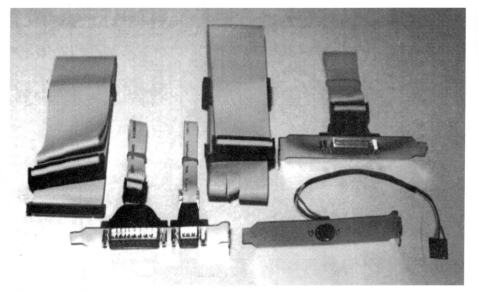

Figure 3.40 Here's all the connecting cables that you'll use to attach peripherals to the motherboard

STEP 13   Install the floppy drive

The front panel of your case has several removable plastic or metal plates covering the drive bays. The narrow plates cover the bays for 3.5" drives while the wider plates cover the bays for 5.25" drives.

These plates can be removed from the front panel by gently popping them out from the front panel. Remove one of the plates for your 3.5" floppy drive as in Figure 3.41.

Next slide the floppy drive into one of the 3.5" bays so that the front of the drive is flush with the front as in Figure 3.42. Then secure the drive to the case with at least four screws. You may have to flip the case on its other side to secure both sides of the drive to the mounting brackets.

A 34-wire ribbon cable is used to connect the floppy drive to the motherboard (or I/O card). In Figure 3.43, you can see that one end of the cable connects to the floppy controller on either the motherboard or a separate I/O board.

Figure 3.41 Remove the face plate from the front cover of the case

The other end has two connectors for the A drive. One of these is for a floppy drive that has an edge connector and the other is for a floppy drive that has a 34-pin connector. See Figure 3.44.

In the middle are two connectors for the B drive. Again, one is for an edge connector and the other for a 34-pin connector.

Figure 3.42 Slide the floppy drive into the case from the front

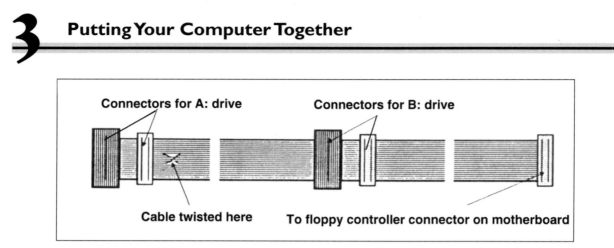

Figure 3.43 A 34-wire ribbon cable connects floppy drive to the motherboard or I/O board

Most likely, your floppy drive will have a 34-pin connector since the edge connectors are ancient. In any case, plug either the 34-pin connector or the edge connector into the back of the floppy drive. The edge connector on the ribbon is "keyed" so it will fit onto the floppy drive in only one direction. Then plug one of the power supply connectors into the back of the floppy drive as in Figure 3.45.

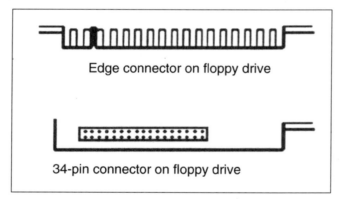

Figure 3.44 The two types of connectors on the back of a floppy drive

Along the length of the cable is a color line which indicates pin 1 on the connector. Plug the 34-pin connector into the floppy controller port on the motherboard (or separate I/O board) making sure that pin 1 of the connector matches pin 1 on the board. See Figure 3.46.

Figure 3.45 Plug the power supply cable and the 34-pin connector (A-drive) into the floppy drive

Figure 3.46 Plug the 34-pin ribbon cable from the floppy drive to the motherboard (or separate I/O card)

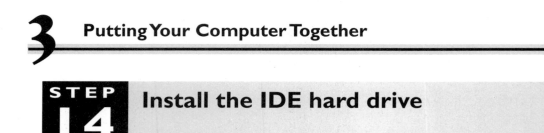

Install the IDE hard drive

Since the hard drive will be totally enclosed within the case, you won't have to remove a plastic or metal plate from the case's front panel to install your hard drive. Slide the hard drive into one of the bays so that the connectors on the drive are accessible. Secure the hard drive to the case with four screws.

A 40-wire ribbon cable is used to connect the hard drive to the motherboard (or I/O card). The ribbon cable has three 40-pin connectors - one at each end and a third about one-third of the way towards one end as in Figure 3.47.

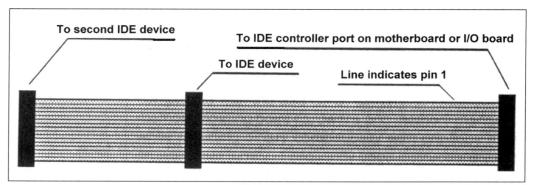

Figure 3.47 A 40-wire ribbon cable connects IDE devices to the motherboard or I/O board

Plug the other end of the cable into connector on the hard drive, again making sure that pin 1 on the cable matches pin 1 of the hard drive. Plug one of the power supply connectors into the hard drive as in Figure 3.48.

A color line (usually red) along the length of the cable ribbon indicates pin 1, similar to the 34-pin floppy cable. Plug one end of the 40-pin connectors into the primary IDE controller connector on the motherboard (or separate I/O board) making sure that pin 1 of the connector matches pin 1 on the board as in Figure 3.49.

Figure 3.48 Plug the 40-pin connector and the power supply connector into the back of the hard drive

Figure 3.49 Plug the 40-pin connector into the motherboard (or separate I/O card)

Install the IDE CD-ROM drive

Remove one of the plastic or metal plates from the front panel that covers a 5.25" bay. Regardless of the make of an IDE CD-ROM drive, they are configured similarly. To be absolutely sure, you'll want to refer to the CD-ROM drive installation manual. Our explanation is a general one, but it should be similar to that from your installation manual.

An IDE device - hard drive or CD-ROM drive - is set to a master device or a slave device by setting a jumper on the rear of the drive. If the IDE controller port already has one device attached (our computer already has the hard drive connected), then that device (the hard drive) is the master and the second device (the CD-ROM) is the slave. Therefore you set the jumper on the CD-ROM drive which makes it a slave. This is usually the default setting from the factory.

After you set the jumper, slide the CD-ROM drive into the bay so that the front of the CD-ROM drive is flush with the front. Secure the CD-ROM drive to the case with four screws. Locate the middle 40-pin connector on the ribbon cable and plug it into the back of the CD-ROM drive as you align pin 1 of the connector to pin 1 of the CD-ROM drive. Plug a 4-wire power cable into the power connector on the CD-ROM drive. See Figure 3.50.

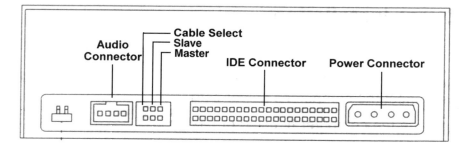

Figure 3.50 The back of a typical IDE CD-ROM drive

Alternative:

You can also connect the CD-ROM to the secondary IDE controller port. If no other devices are connected to the secondary IDE controller, then you would set the jumper on the CD-ROM drive which makes it a master. Some manufacturers recommend that you use this setup so the performance of a hard drive sharing the same cable is not adversely affected by the slower CD-ROM transfer rate. If you choose this method, you must use a second 40-pin ribbon cable and plug one connector into the secondary IDE port and the other end into the CD-ROM drive.

In order to hear audio through your sound card, you'll have to connect the CD-ROM drive to the sound card with an audio cable. One end of the cable attaches to the rear of the CD-ROM drive and the other plugs into the sound card.

Install the video display card

This motherboard has four PCI slots (white) and four ISA/EISA slots (brown). Since we have selected a PCI video display card, we'll insert the card into one of the PCI slots. Secure the card to the back of the case with a screw.

Figure 3.51 Inserting the video display card into a PCI slot

Like most others, you do not have to change any settings on this video display card.

STEP 17 Install sound card

Because we've selected a Plug 'n' Play sound card, there aren't any jumpers or switches that we have to set on this card.

If you are installing a conventional sound card (not Plug 'n Play), then you may have to set jumpers or switches so that the operation of the sound card does not interfere with the operation of any other devices connected to the computer. Since there are so many different sound cards, we can't tell you how to configure any particular sound card, but the default settings are often a good place to start. Creative Labs Sound Blaster and compatible cards usually have a default of I/O port address 220, IRQ 5, DMA 1 which usually work well.

Insert the sound card into one of the ISA slots. Secure the card to back of the case with a screw. Plug the speakers into the sound card.

Refer to the sound card installation manual to locate the CD audio connector. Plug the audio cable from the CD-ROM into the CD audio connector on the sound card.

Connect the mouse port to the motherboard

This motherboard has a connector for a PS/2 style mouse port.

The PS/2 style connector for the mouse is mounted onto a metal expansion slot cover. A narrow ribbon cable (or wire harness) runs between this connector and the motherboard.

Plug the six pin connector into the appropriate connector on the motherboard (for our motherboard it's J10) making sure that pin 1 on the motherboard corresponds to pin 1 on the connector (colored line indicates pin 1). Next mount the expansion slot cover with the mouse port onto the back panel of the case as in Figure 3.52.

Finally, plug the mouse into the mouse port as in Figure 3.53:

Figure 3.52 Securing the mouse port to the case

Figure 3.53 Plug the mouse in the PS/2 mouse port

Connect the serial ports to motherboard

This motherboard has built in I/O capabilities. If you're using a separate I/O card, then you'll also have these same I/O capabilities.

Figure 3.54   Securing a 9-pin serial port connector to the back of the case

Part of these capabilities include two serial communication ports. Both of the serial ports mount on the back panel of the case. There are usually removable knockouts on the back panel for various connectors. The connectors are either the smaller 9-pin connector or the larger 25-pin connector. Both are male gender. Remove one or both of the knockouts for the desired connector size.

Mount the metal connector(s) to the case with two hex screws as in Figure 3.54. A flat ribbon runs between this connector and attaches to the motherboard (or separate I/O board) with a 10-pin plastic connector. The motherboard connectors are usually clearly labeled. Plug the connector into either the COM1 or COM2 connectors. Be sure that pin 1 on the motherboard corresponds to pin 1 on the cable (colored line indicates pin 1).

The serial port is now ready for use.

STEP 20   Connect the parallel port to the motherboard

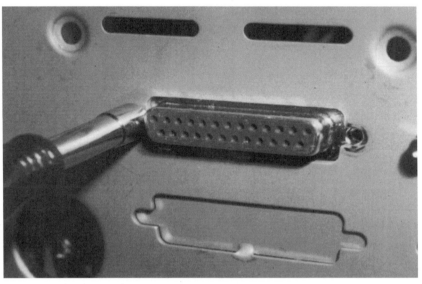

Figure 3.55   Secure the parallel port connector to the back of the case

In addition to the two serial ports, the I/O capabilities of this motherboard (or separate I/O card) include a parallel port - sometimes called a printer port.

The parallel port is a 25-pin female connector that usually mounts onto the back panel of the case. Remove one of the knockouts for this connector size.

Mount the connector to the back panel of the case as in Figure 3.55. A flat ribbon runs between this connector and attaches to the motherboard with a 26 pin plastic connector. The motherboard connectors are usually clearly labeled with the word PARALLEL or PRINTER or LPT. Be sure that pin 1 on the motherboard corresponds to pin 1 on the cable (colored line indicates pin 1).

The parallel port is now ready for use.

Connect the monitor to the video display card

We installed the video display card in our computer system in Step 16.

The 15-pin connector for the monitor is now at the back panel of the case. Plug the monitor cable into the video display card connector.

Finally, plug the monitor power cord into a grounded electrical outlet.

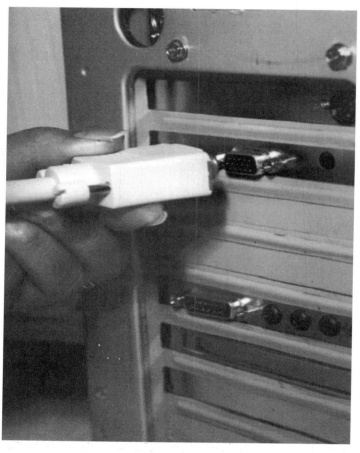

Figure 3.56 Connecting the monitor

Connect the keyboard

The keyboard connector is attached directly to the motherboard. When you mount the motherboard in the case, the connector is aligned with a cutout in the case.

Plug the keyboard into the connector as in the following figure:

Figure 3.57 Plug the keyboard cable into the keyboard connector on the back of the case

STEP 23 — Check and Double Check the Connections. Clean up.

We're almost ready to turn on the computer. But first, we're asking you to carefully inspect and review your work.

Go back and review Step 5 through Step 22.

This may seem like an unnecessary thing to do, but by rereading and inspecting your work, you will help insure that you've done things correctly. Things that you want to especially look for:

❖ Make sure that the bottom side of the motherboard is not touching any metal parts.

❖ Look for loose wires that may be touching the motherboard. A short circuit can damage the system.

❖ Move unused power supply connectors away from other components. You can rubber band these to hold them out of the way.

STEP 24 Turn on the Power

You're now ready to try out the new computer.

We assume that the hard drive is a brand new one that has not been formatted and does not contain an operating system.

Remove any diskettes from the floppy drive.

Turn on the power to the monitor.

Next, turn on the power to the computer.

When we turned our computer on, first the video display card BIOS displays this message:

> © 1995 Number Nine Visual Technology Corp
> All rights reserved
> #9-868 BIOS version 2.04.03

Then the BIOS on the motherboard displays these messages:

> Award Modular BIOS V4.50PG. An Energy Star Ally
> Copyright © 1994-95, Award Software, Inc.
>
> 03/13/1996 For i430HX PCIset
>
> PENTIUM-S CPU at 166MHz
> Memory Test: 16384K OK
>
> Award Plug and Play BIOS Extension v1.0A
> Copyright © 1995, Award Software, Inc.
>   Detecting HDD Primary Master WDC AC2120

Since this hard drive is brand new and is not yet formatted, the following message was displayed on the screen telling us that the BIOS is not able to load the operating system from the hard drive.

> DISK BOOT FAILURE, INSERT SYSTEM DISK AND PRESS ENTER

Even though we haven't progressed very far, we have verified that the computer system is up and running. Make sure that the CPU cooling fan is <u>operating correctly</u>. If not, turn off the power and recheck the connections to the power supply.

Here's this startup screens for a second computer that we build.. In this computer system, we used a Trident video display card. When we turned the power on, the video display card BIOS did not display any messages on the screen. We went directly the messages from the motherboard BIOS:

```
Award Modular BIOS V4.50PG. An Energy Star Ally
Copyright © 1994-95, Award Software, Inc.


P5I437/250A BIOS V1.0 96-4-33


PENTIUM-S CPU at 166MHz
Memory Test:  16384K OK


Award Plug and Play BIOS Extension v1.0A
Copyright © 1995, Award Software, Inc.
  Detecting HDD Primary Master  WDC AC2120
```

Again, the hard drive does not contain a bootable operating system, so we see the following message:

```
DISK BOOT FAILURE, INSERT SYSTEM DISK AND PRESS ENTER
```

Even though we get these error messages, we have verified that the computer is working properly.

Success! Both of these computer systems are working. We can now move on. If you're still having trouble see the next page.

Before we move on to the final step on installing the operating system to the hard drive, you can now complete the assembly by closing the case. Carefully slide the cover onto the case and secure it with the hex screws reversing the process of Step 3.

Now let's move to the final step of installing the operating system on the hard drive.

If You Have Trouble

Screen is blank when the system is turned on:

Things to check

- ❖ Power supply is not plugged into an electrical outlet
- ❖ Monitor is not plugged into electrical outlet
- ❖ Monitor is not turned on
- ❖ Monitor is not connected to the video display card
- ❖ Video display card is not properly seated in the motherboard slot
- ❖ SIMMs are not properly seated in their sockets
- ❖ SIMMs are not installed in pairs
- ❖ Motherboard is not connected to power supply (P8 and P9 connectors)
- ❖ Floppy cable is not properly connected to the floppy drive
- ❖ Floppy cable is not properly connected to the motherboard (or I/O card)
- ❖ Hard drive cable is not properly connected to the hard drive
- ❖ Hard drive cable is not properly connected to the motherboard (or I/O card)
- ❖ Motherboard not grounded to the case. Make sure that the motherboard is firmly secured to the case using brass standoffs

Screen displays BIOS startup message but then "hangs" before DOS is loaded

Things to check

- ❖ Hard drive is not plugged into IDE port
- ❖ Power cable is not plugged into the hard drive
- ❖ Power cable is not plugged into the floppy drive
- ❖ Floppy drive is not plugged into the floppy controller cable
- ❖ Floppy controller cable is plugged in backwards
- ❖ Floppy drive is plugged into "B" connector instead of "A"
- ❖ Hard drive controller cable is plugged in backwards
- ❖ Boot sequence for the hard drive should be A,C so it will load DOS from floppy drive This is specified by using BIOS setup. For our computer, to enter BIOS setup, press Del as the system is starting

4

Installing Your Operating System

4 Installing Your Operating System

N ow that the computer system is working, we still have to install the operating system. With all of the power in our new Pentium, we have the hardware to run Windows 95.

To install Windows 95, we're going to take an approach that keeps installation problems to a minimum. We've used the following method to install and reinstall Windows 95 on many computers. It isn't the most direct route to Windows 95, but it is very effective.

Our approach is to get both the CD-ROM drive and sound card to work under DOS. After we do this, then we are pretty much assured that they will also work under Windows 95.

To install Windows 95 we'll use the following:

1. Boot diskette containing either the DOS 5 or DOS 6 operating system. The diskette must be bootable and contain the following files:

   COMMAND.COM

   IO.SYS

   MSDOS.SYS

   FDISK.COM

   FORMAT.COM

   SYS.COM

   MSCDEX.EXE

2. Installation diskette for your CD-ROM drive

3. Installation diskette for your sound card

4. Windows 95 CD-ROM.

Here's an outline of how we're going to install Windows 95 onto your new computer:

1. Boot the computer using the bootable diskette from floppy drive A:

2. Partition the hard drive to make space for an operating system

3. Format the hard drive and copy the MS-DOS operating system to it

4. Copy the other files from the floppy diskette to the hard drive

5. Install the software to access the CD-ROM drive

6. Install the software for the sound card

7. Install Windows 95 from the CD-ROM

So let's get started.

Insert the bootable MS-DOS floppy diskette into drive A:

Turn on the computer

MS-DOS will load from the floppy and display the **A:>** prompt.

At the prompt type:

```
A:> fdisk  Enter
```

The FDISK program will start and you'll see this screen:

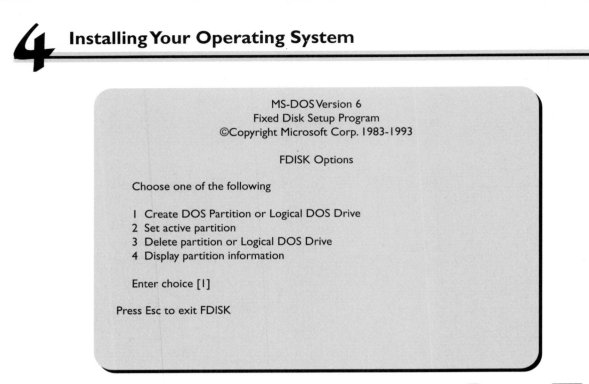

Since we want to create a new DOS partition on this hard drive, type ⊡ and press [Enter].

Now this screen appears:

```
                    MS-DOS Version 6
                 Fixed Disk Setup Program
              ©Copyright Microsoft Corp. 1983-1993

                        FDISK Options

        Choose one of the following

          1  Create Primary DOS partition
          2  Create Extended DOS partition
          3  Create Logical DOS Drive(s) in the Extended DOS partition


        Enter choice [1]

        Press Esc to exit FDISK
```

We need a Primary DOS Partition, so type ⊡ again and press [Enter]. You'll then see the following screen:

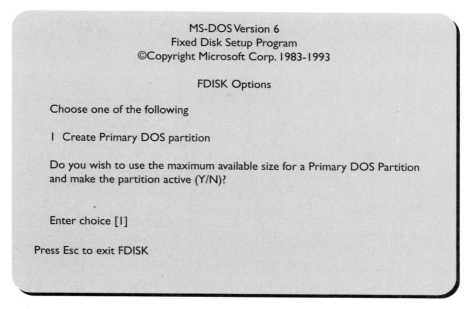

We will use the entire hard drive for the new partition, so type Y and press Enter.

FDISK will allocate the entire hard drive space to the new partition and displays this final message:

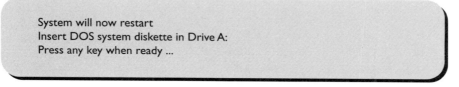

Press any key and DOS will reload from your floppy diskette.

Before we use the hard drive, we first have to format the drive. Type the following, making sure that you include the switch **/s** which transfers the MS-DOS operating system from the floppy diskette to the hard drive:

```
A:> format c: /s  Enter
```

The FORMAT program will start and display this warning message before it writes over any data which may have been previously written to the hard drive:

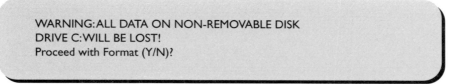

Assuming that this is a new hard drive, no data will be lost, so type Y and press Enter.

The hard drive is then formatted and the minimal MS-DOS system is transferred to the hard drive. When FORMAT is almost done, you'll be asked to enter a label identifier for the newly formatted hard drive:

> Volume Label (11 character, ENTER for none)?

You can type an 11 character name, for example:

```
DRIVE_C Enter
```

Now that the hard drive is formatted, change to that drive:

```
A:>   c: Enter
```

Copy the other files from diskette to the hard drive by typing:

```
A:> copy a:*.* c: Enter
```

Next, remove the floppy diskette from drive A.

Press the reset switch on the case or turn the power off and then back on again to boot the computer from the hard drive. MS-DOS will load again, this time from the hard drive, and display the **C:>** prompt.

```
C:>
```

Now we'll install the software to access the CD-ROM drive. The drivers and setup programs are supplied on a floppy diskette with your CD-ROM drive. You'll probably have to run a program from the diskette named SETUP or INSTALL. The instruction manual for the CD-ROM will tell you the exact name.

Before running the INSTALL program for the Creative Labs 16 Plug 'n Play sound card, we had to install the Plug and Play Configuration Manager. This set of three floppy diskettes is needed for any Plug and Play devices - sound cards, modems, etc. This screen was displayed when we installed the PnP Configuration Manager:

> Plug and Play for MS-DOS® and Windows ™ Configuration Manager - R1.43
>
> Copyright 1993, 1994, 1995 Intel Corporation ALL RIGHTS RESERVED
>
> MS-DOS is a registered trademark and Windows is a trademark of Microsoft Corp.
>
> Found Plug and Play ISA card: Creative SB16 PnP
>
> The Plug and Play ISA card has been successfully configured

After Plug and Play installation, we can install the sound card software. The setup program is supplied on a floppy diskette for our sound card. You'll probably have to run a program from the diskette named SETUP or INSTALL. The instruction manual for the sound card will tell you the exact name.

Reboot the computer to try out the sound card.

With the CD-ROM and the sound card successfully installed, we can now install Windows 95.

Insert the Windows 95 CD-ROM into the CD-ROM drive. Change to the CD-ROM drive by typing thee following:

```
D: Enter
```

Now start the Windows 95 installation by typing:

```
D:>  setup  Enter
```

The Windows 95 installation will begin. Follow the directions on the screen to install a full version of Windows 95. When installation is complete, you will be asked to reboot your computer. Now you're on your own!!!

CONGRATULATIONS. You've graduated from computer building school and are ready to start using your brand new Pentium PC with Windows 95.

5

Getting More Information

5 Getting More Information

Books

Upgrading & Maintaining your PC, 4th Edition written by Schueller and Veddler; published by Abacus, 1996, ISBN 1-55755-300-9, $34.95 w/ CD-ROM

Win95 Rx written by Kober, Buechel and Baecker; published by Abacus, 1996, ISBN 1-55755-297-5, $34.95 w/CD-ROM

Upgrading and Repairing PCs, 5th Edition written by Scott Mueller; published by Que, 1995, ISBN 0-7897-0321-1, $49.95 w/CD-ROM

The Winn L. Rosch Hardware Bible, 3rd Edition written by Winn Rosch; published by SAMs Publishing, 1994, ISBN 1-56686-127-6, $35.00.

Upgrade & Maintain your PC written by James Karney; published by MID Press, ISBN 1-55828-294-7, 1994, $34.95 w/diskette

The Complete PC Upgrade & Maintenance Guide written by Mark Minasi; published by Sybex, 1993, $24.95.

Other References

Byte Magazine
One Phoenix Mill Lane
Peterborough, NH 03458
Phone (603) 924-9281
Toll free (800) 257-9402
Fax (603) 924-2550
http://www.byte.com

Compu-Mart Magazine
899 Presidential
Suite 110
Richardson, TX 75081
Phone (214) 238-1133
Toll free (800) 864-1155
Fax (214) 238-1132

Computer Direct
P.O. Box 55886
Birmingham, AL 35255
Phone (205) 988-9708
Toll free (800) 366-0676
Fax (205) 987-3237

Computer Shopper
One Park Avenue
New York, NY 10016
Phone (212) 503-3900
Toll free (800) 274-6384
Fax (212) 503-3995

Nuts & Volts Magazine
430 Princeland Court
Corona, CA 91719
Phone (909) 371-8497
Toll free (800) 783-4624
Fax (909) 371-3052
http://www.nutsvolts.com

PC Novice Magazine
P.O. Box 85380
Lincoln, NE 68501
Toll Free (800) 472-3500

Processor
P.O. Box 85518
Lincoln, NE 68501
Phone (402) 479-2141
Toll Free (800) 334-7443
Fax (402) 477-9252

Software Tools And Diagnostics

First Aid 95 Deluxe

Software that detects and fixes hundreds of Windows 95 problems.

> CyberMedia Inc.
> 3000 Ocean Park Blvd
> Suite 2001
> Santa Monica, CA 90405
> Phone (310) 581-4700
> Fax (310) 581-4720
> http://www.cybermedia.com

Micro-Scope 6.1

Software that helps you diagnose problems with a PC. This software is works regardless of the operating system which may be installed and checks CPU, memory, IRQs, DMAs, BIOS, hard drives, floppy drives, video cards, more.

> Micro 2000
> 1100 E Broadway
> Suite 301
> Glendale, CA 91205
> Toll-free (800) 864-8008
> Phone (818) 547-0125
> Fax (818) 547-0397
> http://www.micro2000.com

PC Snoop

A hard disk and floppy disk diagnostic and repair utility

> Computer Intelligence Corp
> 42015 Ford Rd
> Suite 262
> Canton, MI 48187-3529
> Phone (313) 981-9630
> Fax (313) 981-9634
> http://www.adcomm.com/pcsnoop/

Post-Probe

A plug-in card that helps to troubleshoot problems in "dead" PCs. The LEDs on the card identify problem areas.

Micro 2000
1100 E Broadway
Suite 301
Glendale, CA 91205
Toll-free (800) 864-8008
Phone (818) 547-0125
Fax (818) 547-0397
http://www.micro2000.com

Manufacturers And Suppliers

Where can I buy components?

There are loads of places which sell computer components.

Computer Stores

Most local computer stores build custom computers to order. These local computer stores also sell components. Many times these components are of the *OEM* variety, that is they are not packaged in fancy boxes, but are bulk packed to reduce costs. The quality of these components is usually as high as the equivalent retail packaged components.

Computer Superstores

Computer "superstores" such as Best Buy, Circuit City, CompUSA, ElekTek, Frys, Micro Center and others also sell components. These stores usually sell retail packaged components and are noted for competitive prices and quality products and have standard return policies for defective merchandise.

Computer Shows

Another attractive place to buy components is at one of the many computer shows. These are sometimes called expos, fairs, flea markets or swap meets and are held in many cities nationwide - usually on weekends. At these shows, dozens of small hardware and software vendors sell everything from ink refill kits and paper for your printer, to motherboards, memory, add-on cards and complete computer systems, often at deeply discounted prices.

Since most of these vendors participate in the shows regularly and welcome repeat business, they stand behind the quality and performance of the components which they sell. As is the case with all purchases, don't buy a component based solely on its price. Rather, buy a component because it meets your exact requirements and because you feel that a given vendor can meet those needs satisfactorily.

Check your local newspapers and computer bulletin boards for the location of these shows.

Mail Order / Phone Order

You can also buy components from mail order firms. An especially large source of mail order companies is found in "rags" such as Computer Shopper and Nuts & Volts. Other monthly magazines have extensive ads from components suppliers. Check these publications to find a list of mail order (and toll free 800 number) hardware component dealers. You can usually buy those "hard to find" components from many of the mail order electronic parts suppliers.

On the next pages is a list of manufacturers and suppliers of components and accessories which you may contact to find out more about their products.

Abrams Computer Industries

444 Lake Cook Road
Suite 1
Deerfield, IL 60015
Phone (847) 267-0644
Fax (847) 940-7715
Supplier of motherboards, CPUs (including Cyrix 6x86), memory

Acer Labs

4701 Patrick Henry Drive
Santa Clara, Ca 95054
Phone (408) 764-0644
Fax (408) 496-6142
http://www.acer.com
Motherboards and chipsets

Advanced Integration Research

2188 Del Franco Street
San Jose, CA 95131
Phone (408) 428-0800
Fax (408) 428-0950
http://www.airwebs.com
Manufacturer of motherboards

Alltech Electronics

2618 Temple Heights
Oceanside, CA 92056
Phone (619) 724-2404
Fax (619) 724-8808
http://www.allelec.com
Supplier of electronics components and parts

Alltronics

2300 Zanker Road
San Jose, CA 95131
Phone (408) 943-9773
Fax (408) 943-9776
http://www.alltronics.com
Supplier of electronics components and parts

Alternative Computer Solutions

Naperville, IL 60565
Phone (708) 420-9921
Fax (708) 420-9312
Supplier of memory

AMD Corporation

One AMD Place
Sunnyvale, CA 94088
Phone (408) 749-5703
Fax (408) 774-7024
http://www.amd.com
Manufacturer of CPUs

American Megatrends International

6145-F Northbelt Pkwy
Norcross, GA 30071
Phone (770) 246-8600
Toll free 800-U-BUY-AMI
Fax (770) 246-8790
http://www.megatrends.com
BIOS

Amtech Computers

4005 Carpenter Road

Ypsilanti, MI 48197

Phone (313) 677-6868

Fax (313) 677-8778

Supplier of motherboards, CPUs, memory, add-on cards, cases, peripherals

A.R.E. Electronics

15272 State Route 12 East

Findlay, OH 45840

Phone (419) 422-1588

Fax (419) 422-4432

Supplier of cables, connectors, tools, switch boxes, hardware.

Astra Computer Corp.

4803 Donald Avenue

Richmond Hts, OH 44143

Phone (216) 691-9551

Fax (216) 691-9756

Supplier of motherboards, CPUs, memory, add-on cards, peripherals, cases

ASUS Computers International

721 Charcot Avenue

San Jose, CA 95131

Phone (408) 474-0567

Fax (408) 474-0568

http://www.asus.com

Manufacturer of motherboards

Avery Distributors

3685 Stone School Rd

Ann Arbor, MI 48108

Phone (313) 677-5844

gersha@aol.com

Supplier of memory

Award Software International

777 East Middlefield Rd

Mountain View, CA 94043

Phone (415) 968-4433

Fax (415) 968-0774

http://www.award.com

BIOS

Compuparts Laboratory, Inc.

201 E Cripe Street

South Bend, IN 46637

Phone (219) 243-0421

Fax (219) 243-0422

Supplier motherboards, CPUs, memory, add-on cards

Cyrix Corporation

P.O. Box 850118

Richardson, TX 75085

Phone (214) 968-8388

Toll free (800) 462-9749

Fax (214) 699-9857

http://www.cyrix.com

Manufacturer of CPUs

Digi-Key Corp.

701 Brooks Ave South

Thief River, MN 56701

Toll-free (800) 334-4530

Fax (218) 681-3380

Supplier of connectors, cables, tools, electronic components and switches.

Digilink Technology

3050 Lake Lansing Rd

Suite B

East Lansing, MI 48823

Tel (517) 333-9888

Fax (517) 333-9988

Supplier of motherboards, memory, add-on cards, peripherals, cases

Discount Computer, Inc.

10021 Telegraph Road

Redford, MI 48239

Phone (313) 531-3241

Fax (313) 531-1717

Supplier of motherboards, memory, add-on cards, peripherals, cases

DTK Ltd

1035 Centennial Avenue

Picataway, NJ 08854

Phone (908) 562-8800

Fax (908) 562-8400

http://www.dtk.com

Manufacturer of BIOs and motherboards

D.W. Technologies

P.O. Box 4061

Dearborn, MI 48126

Phone (313) 361-6939

Fax (313) 361-6939

Supplier of motherboards, CPUs, memory, add-on cards, peripherals.

Expert Computer

14510 11 Mile Road

Warren, MI 48089

Phone (810) 445-6133

Fax (810) 455-6132

Supplier of motherboards, CPUs, memory, add-on cards, peripherals, cases

GPC Computers

2240 28th Street SE

Grand Rapids, MI 49508

Phone (616) 452-8948

Fax (616) 452-8819

Supplier of motherboards, CPUs, memory, add-on cards, peripherals, cases

Halted Electronics Supply

3500 Ryder Street

Santa Clara, CA 95051

Phone (408) 732-1573

Toll free (800) 442-3833

Fax (408) 732-6428

http://www.halted.com

Supplier of electronics components and parts

Hi-Tech Business Machines

5324 West 79th Street
Indianapolis, IN 46268
Phone (317) 872-6658
Toll free (800) 335-8302
http://www.hi-tech.net
Memory, add-on cards, peripherals, cases.

Intel Corporation

2200 Mission College Blvd
Santa Clara, CA 95052
Phone (408) 528-4725
Fax (408) 765-9904
Manufacturer of CPUs and chipsets

IQ's Technology

15417 West Warren
Dearborn, MI 48126
Phone (313) 581-0506
Fax (313) 581-8841
Supplier of motherboards, memory, add-on cards, peripherals, cases.

JDR Microdevices

1850 South 10th Street
San Jose, CA 95112-4108
Phone (408) 494-1400
Toll free (800) 538-5000
Fax (408) 494-1420
Supplier of hardware, cases, power supplies, keyboards, cables, tools, networking

JK Lee Corporation

1198 E. Dundee Road
Palatine, IL 60067
Phone (847) 358-7115
Fax (847) 358-7115
Supplier of memory and CPUs

M Technologies Inc

1931 Hartog Drive
San Jose, CA 95131
Phone (408) 441-8818
http://www.mtiusa.com
Manufacturer of motherboards

MCM Electronics

650 Congress Park Dr
Centerville, OH 45459-4072
Phone (513) 434-0031
Toll free (800) 543-4330
Fax (513) 434-6959
Supplier of hardware, cases, power supplies, keyboards, cables, tools, networking, electronics parts

Marvic International Inc.

768 East 93rd Street
Brooklyn, NY 11236
Phone (718) 346-7822
Toll Free (800) 678-8128
Fax (718) 346-0438
Supplier of hardware, cases, power supplies, keyboards, cables, tools, networking

Microid Research

2336-D Walsh Ave
Santa Clara, CA 95051
http://www.mrbios.com
Manufacturers of BIOS

Microland Computers

9509 N. Milwaukee Ave
Niles, IL 60714
Phone (847) 966-2300
Fax (847) 966-2368
Supplier of motherboards, CPUs, add-on cards

Norton Computer Sytems, Inc.

4129 W Saginaw
Lansing, MI 48917
Phone (517) 323-3170
Fax (517) 323-2495
Supplier of cables, connectors, tools, switch boxes, hardware.

Opti, Inc.

2525 Walsh Avenue
Santa Clara, Ca 95051
Phone (408) 980-8174
Fax (408) 980-8860
http://www.opti.com
Chipsets

Phoenix Technologies Ltd

2770 De La Cruz
Santa Clara, CA 95050
Phone (408) 654-9000
Fax (408) 452-1985
http://www.ptldt.com
BIOS

Prime Electronic Components

150 West Industry Court
Deer Park, NY 11729
Phone (516) 254-0101
Fax (516) 242-8995
http://www.imsworld.com/prime/
Supplier of electronics components and parts

RA Enterprises

2260 De La Cruz Blvd
Santa Clara, CA 95050
Phone (408) 986-8286
Toll free (800) 801-0230
Fax (408) 986-1009
Supplier of electronics components and parts

Sam's Computers

5218 Wilson Mills Road
Cleveland, OH 44143
Phone (216) 449-1107
Fax (216) 449-3795
Supplier of motherboards, CPUs, memory, add-on cards

Silicon Integrated Systems (SIS)

204 North Wolfe Road
Sunnyvale, CA 94086
Phone (408) 730-5600
Fax (408) 730-5639
Manufacturer of chipsets

Skyline Computerware

3749 Grand Blvd
Brookfield, IL 60513
Phone (708) 387-1064
Fax (708) 387-1063
Supplier of standoffs and other small hardware, cooling fans, cables, add-on cards

Sky-Tech Computers

28480 Southfield Road
Lathrup Village, MI 48076
Phone (810) 559-6932
Fax (810) 559-0827
Supplier of motherboards, CPUs, memory, add-on cards, peripherals, cases

Southgate Computers

15125 Eureka
Southgate, MI 48195
Toledo, OH 43606
Phone (313) 282-6133
Fax (313) 282-9079

Super Micro

2178 Paragon Drive
San Jose, Ca 95131
Phone (408) 451-1118
Fax (408) 451-1110
http://www.supermicro.com
Manufacturer of motherboards

The Computer Connection

401 N. Main Street
Polk, OH 44866
Phone (419) 945-2877
Fax (419) 945-1342
Supplier of motherboards, CPUs, memory, add-on cards, peripherals, cases

Tynan Computers

1753 S. Main Street
San Jose, CA 95035
Phone (408) 956-8000
Fax (408) 956-8044
http://www.tynan.com
Manufacturer of motherboards

Wintergreen Systems, Inc.

3315 W. 96th Street
Indianapolis, IN 46268
Phone (317) 872-1974
Fax (317) 872-4686
//http:www.in.net/wsi
Supplier of motherboards, CPUs, memory, add-on cards

6

Shopping Check List

6 Shopping Check List

So, you think you're ready to go shopping?

On the next pages, we've made a shopping list. This list will help you organize the features that you want for each of the major components in your system.

You may want to make multiple copies of this list.

CPU (circle desired processor)	Vendor A	Vendor B	Vendor C
Pentium processors P100 P120 P133 P150 P166 P200 **Cyrix 6x86 processors** P100+ P120+ P133+ P150+ P166+	$_____	$_____	$_____

Motherboard select features	Motherboard A		Motherboard B		Motherboard C	
CPU speed to 200 MHz?	❏ Yes	❏ No	❏ Yes	❏ No	❏ Yes	❏ No
Maximum RAM to 128MB?	❏ Yes	❏ No	❏ Yes	❏ No	❏ Yes	❏ No
Handles EDO memory?	❏ Yes	❏ No	❏ Yes	❏ No	❏ Yes	❏ No
Bus type (PCI is recommended)	❏ PCI	❏ VLB	❏ PCI	❏ VLB	❏ PCI	❏ VLB
# of PCI or VLB slots						
# of ISA slots						
Cache memory capacity (min. 256K)	❏ Onboard	❏ Separate	❏ Onboard	❏ Separate	❏ Onboard	❏ Separate
I/O on MB or separate I/O card	❏ Onboard	❏ Separate	❏ Onboard	❏ Separate	❏ Onboard	❏ Separate
EIDE for 4 fixed drives	❏ Yes	❏ No	❏ Yes	❏ No	❏ Yes	❏ No
2 floppy drives	❏ Yes	❏ No	❏ Yes	❏ No	❏ Yes	❏ No
2 serial ports (16551 comp.)	❏ Yes	❏ No	❏ Yes	❏ No	❏ Yes	❏ No
1 game port	❏ Yes	❏ No	❏ Yes	❏ No	❏ Yes	❏ No
1 PS/2 mouse port	❏ Yes	❏ No	❏ Yes	❏ No	❏ Yes	❏ No
BIOS						
Plug 'n Play?	❏ Yes	❏ No	❏ Yes	❏ No	❏ Yes	❏ No
Flash?	❏ Yes	❏ No	❏ Yes	❏ No	❏ Yes	❏ No
Model						
Price	$_____		$_____		$_____	

Main memory RAM	Vendor A			Vendor B			Vendor C		
Type: 72-pin standard (FPM) 72-pin EDO	❏ FPM	❏ EDO		❏ FPM	❏ EDO		❏ FPM	❏ EDO	
Parity?	❏ Yes	❏ No		❏ Yes	❏ No		❏ Yes	❏ No	
Amount 8MB 2 x 4MB SIMMs 16MB 2 x 8MB SIMMs 32MB 2 x 16MB SIMMs	❏ 8 MB	❏ 16 MB	❏ 32 MB	❏ 8 MB	❏ 16 MB	❏ 32 MB	❏ 8 MB	❏ 16 MB	❏ 32 MB
Price	$_____			$_____			$_____		

Cache memory (if not onboard)	Vendor C		Vendor C		Vendor C	
Type COAST or SRAM	❏ COAST	❏ SRAM	❏ COAST	❏ SRAM	❏ COAST	❏ SRAM
Capacity (usually 256K)						
Price	$_____		$_____		$_____	

CPU cooling fan		CPU Fan A	CPU Fan B	CPU Fan C
Model				
Price		$_____	$_____	$_____

Case		Case A		Case B		Case C	
Desktop or Tower		❏ Desktop	❏ Tower	❏ Desktop	❏ Tower	❏ Desktop	❏ Tower
Power supply (230 watt minimum)							
Price		$_____		$_____		$_____	

Keyboard		Keyboard A	Keyboard B	Keyboard C
Style				
Model				
Price		$_____	$_____	$_____

Mouse		Mouse A	Mouse B	Mouse C
Style				
Model				
Price		$_____	$_____	$_____

Video display card	Video card A			Video card B			Video card C		
PCI or VLB	❏ PCI	❏ VLB		❏ PCI	❏ VLB		❏ PCI	❏ VLB	
DRAM or VRAM	❏ DRAM	❏ VRAM		❏ DRAM	❏ VRAM		❏ DRAM	❏ VRAM	
Amount of video memory	❏ 1 MB	❏ 2 MB	❏ 4 MB	❏ 1 MB	❏ 2 MB	❏ 4 MB	❏ 1 MB	❏ 2 MB	❏ 4 MB
Model									
Price	$_____			$_____			$_____		

Monitor		Monitor A		Monitor B		Monitor C	
Screen size viewing area							
Dot pitch (.28 minimum)							
Refresh rate (70MHz minimum)							
Interlace or non-interlace		❏ Interlace	❏ NI	❏ Interlace	❏ NI	❏ Interlace	❏ NI
Maximum resolution (600 x 800 minimum)							
Energy saving features		❏ Yes	❏ No	❏ Yes	❏ No	❏ Yes	❏ No
Model							
Price		$_____		$_____		$_____	

Sound card		Sound card A		Sound card B		Sound card C	
Plug 'n' Play		❏ Yes	❏ No	❏ Yes	❏ No	❏ Yes	❏ No
Model							
Price		$_____		$_____		$_____	

Floppy drive	Floppy drive A		Floppy drive B		Floppy drive C	
3.5" drive	❏ Yes	❏ No	❏ Yes	❏ No	❏ Yes	❏ No
5.25" drive	❏ Yes	❏ No	❏ Yes	❏ No	❏ Yes	❏ No
Model						
Price	$_____		$_____		$_____	

IDE hard drive	IDE hard drive A	IDE hard drive B	IDE hard drive C
Capacity (1GB or higher)			
Access speed (12 ms or less)			
Model			
Price	$_____	$_____	$_____

IDE CD-ROM drive	IDE CD-ROM A	IDE CD-ROM B	IDE CD-ROM C
Access speed (4X speed or higher)			
Model			
Price	$_____	$_____	$_____

Software	Vendor A	Vendor B	Vendor C
MS-DOS 5 or 6.22 on diskette	$_____	$_____	$_____
Windows 95 on CD-ROM	$_____	$_____	$_____

PC Catalog

Order Toll Free:
1-800-451-4319

CD-ROM
Included

**CD-ROM
Included**

PC Intern 6th Edition
The Encyclopedia of System Programming

Hundreds of thousands of programmers worldwide rely on the authoritative information in PC Intern. Now in its eighth year of print, it has been regularly and extensively rewritten to stay on the leading edge of software and computer hardware changes. The information in PC Intern is so indispensable that many readers have faithfully "upgraded" to each new edition of the book. In this sixth major revision, world renowned authors Michael Tischer and Bruno Jennrich prove that programmers can continue to count on PC Intern as their most important reference.

PC Intern has been called the "encyclopedia of PC programming" for some very good reasons: it covers virtually every aspect about the PC—from its architecture and makeup to its built-in components and add-on peripherals. It's written in a no-nonsense, easy to follow style; it's authoritative.

Whether you need to understand ISDN communication, access the CD-ROM drive, use DMA techniques, handle your own IRQs, interface to DLLs or use Win95 common controls, you'll find the answers in PC Intern. Authors Tischer and Jennrich clearly explains the "hows" and the "whys" of system level programming using hundreds of practical and detailed examples. They illustrate their solutions in several languages including C++, assembly language, Pascal and Visual Basic. Every program in the book is also included on the companion CD-ROM so you can quickly "borrow" the code as required for your own programming projects. As you use this book, you'll quickly see why so many readers who program for a living have invested in the legendary PC Intern.

What the programmers say about PC Intern:

"Worth every penny: Great book." — E.M. from Canada

"Excellent reference; clear, concise, accurate."
  — D.B. from Massachusetts

"Leading book in its class; software on CD-ROM is great."
  — R.D. from Georgia

Authors: M. Tischer & B. Jennrich
Item #: B304
ISBN: 1-55755-304-1
SRP: $69.95 US/89.95 CAN
  with CD-ROM

Upgrading and Maintaining Your PC
Fourth Edition

Buying a personal computer is a major investment. Today's ever-changing technology requires that you continue to upgrade if you want to maintain a state of the art system. Innovative developments in hardware and software drive your need for more speed, better hardware, and larger capacities. Upgrading and Maintaining Your PC gives you the knowledge and skill that help you upgrade or maintain your system. You'll save time and money by being able to perform your own maintenance and repairs.

How to upgrade, repair, maintain, and more:

- Hard Drives, Memory, and Battery Replacement
- Sound & Video Cards, CD-ROMs
- Pentium Powerhouses 60-133 MHz, Overdrive Processor
- Large Capacity Hard Drives
- Quad Speed CD-ROM Drives
- Sound Cards—64-bit and Wave Table
- Modems/Fax Cards, ISDN
- AMD, Cyrix, AMI, and Intel Processors
- Operating systems—Dos 6.22, Novell DOS, IBM PC DOS 6.3, OS/2 Warp, and Windows 3.1 to Windows 95

**CD-ROM
Included**

On the CD-ROM:

System Sleuth Analyzer from Dariana ($99.95 value)—A toolbox of valuable PC diagnostic aids rolled into a single, easy to use software utility. It lets you explore exacting details of your PC with our fear of accidental, unrecoverable modifications to a particular subsystem.

Intel's Pentium Chip Test—calculate the now famous math problem" ion your own system.

Cyrix Upgrade Compatibility Test—run "Cyrix's" own test to see if you can upgrade with one of their new chips.

Authors: H. Veddeler & U. Schuller
Item #: B300
ISBN: 1-55755-300-9
SRP: $34.95 US/46.95 CAN
        with CD-ROM

Order Direct Toll Free 1-800-451-4319

In US and Canada add $5.00 shipping and handling. Foreign orders add $13.00 per item.
Michigan residents add 6% sales tax.

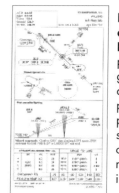